Che … n

The Power of … nce and Attention
to Transform Hospitality

PHILIPPE KRENZER & JANNES SÖRENSEN

Checking In
The Power of Presence and Attention to Transform Hospitality

Published by
Kepler Publishing
London, United Kingdom

ISBN 978-1-0369-5391-1

First published in 2026

STAY HUMAN, LIVE BETTER

This book is dedicated to the memory of my dear friend and co-author, Philippe, whose untimely passing in late October 2025 has left a profound void. Over the past five years, we poured our passion and vision for hospitality into these pages, a journey that spanned fifteen years of collaboration, mentorship, and friendship. Philippe was not just a co-author, but a guiding light and a teacher whose influence permeates every word we wrote.

I am also deeply grateful to Wessel Pretorius, Jacob Mayne and Raphael Pallais for their invaluable conversations on luxury and hospitality, and to Sarah Stein Lubrano and Martine de Geus for their meticulous efforts in organizing and structuring our thoughts. Additionally, my heartfelt thanks go to the many hoteliers who generously shared their insights and guest experiences, enriching our understanding of the guest journey in luxury hospitality.

We hoped that this book serves not as a prescriptive gospel, but as a thoughtful tool in the modern hotelier's toolbox. It is designed to inspire enquiry, encourage reflection, and guide each reader along their own unique journey in defining luxury hospitality. May it spark meaningful questions and foster a deeper understanding of one's own place in this evolving and fascinating industry.

As Philippe would say, true hospitality is not an act of service, but an expression of sincere care for the human being in front of you.

Jannes Sörensen, March 2026

Part One
The World Arrives at Your Front Desk...

Part Two
The Guests We Thought We Knew are...

Part Three
Bringing It Together

WELCOME

A few words before the lights go on.

If you are holding this book, you are already someone who cares.

Cares about your guests. Cares about your team.
Cares, perhaps secretly, about making something beautiful and meaningful in a world that often rewards the opposite.

This is a funny time. So many serious issues and here we are, hoteliers, working in a fragmented industry and yet perhaps tending one of the last places where people can truly come to feel whole, rested and safe.

But what can we do besides doing our best for our guests, our employees and our owners?

As it turns out, quite a lot. And that's exciting.

Because while the world may feel over-crowded, overpriced and underwhelming… inside the four walls of a hotel, a lot is still possible. Outside those walls, too.

This book isn't here to fix you, teach you the One Best Way™, or give you bullet points to energise your Monday meeting. It's here to walk beside you. To say:

> *"We see you. We know this work is hard.*
> *We also think it's sacred."*

This is not a book about operations. It's about orientation.

It asks:

> *What if luxury wasn't a performance, but a practice?*
>
> *What if guests didn't just want comfort, but clarity?*
>
> *What if your job wasn't to impress them, but to gently return them to themselves?*
>
> *And what if, in doing that work well, you got to come back to yourself too?*

In this book, we want to focus on possibilities. On clarity, not just complexity. On what it means to make a difference whether in the course of a single shift, or across an entire business model. Because moving forward requires being crystal clear on what the problems are and knowing which ones matter most to you.

You perform at your best when a problem is well understood, excites you and when you believe you can make a difference.

Ask any young recruit and they'll tell you that doing something meaningful is one of the top three reasons they choose, or stay in, a job. Ask any senior manager and they'll admit the same thing. Though their version is often called a midlife crisis. One thing's for sure: it's never too late to transform your practice and contribute meaningfully.

Each chapter here is almost like its own book, designed to stand alone. So you can read them in or out of order, with a cup of coffee, or between two crises.

Each one begins with a question. And each one tackles a problem, sometimes subtle, sometimes urgent, that's bigger than any one of us.

These aren't issues you solve in a shift or a strategy meeting. They're the kind that ride home with you in the rearview mirror. But that's the point. Taking on something bigger than yourself, something worthy of your care, is where meaning lives. That's where craft becomes calling. Where duty becomes dignity.

We'll explore two world problems that directly impact hoteliers more than those in other industries and five broader issues that shape the lives of your guests and your team. For each, we'll ask what the problem is, why it matters for a hotelier to address and how hoteliers can respond in ways that create a positive impact.

There are seven of them. Seven chapters for the emotionally intelligent hotelier. For the operator who wants to do more than meet KPIs. For the chef who can taste when a sauce was made with a heavy heart. For the GM who still believes that hospitality is one of the noblest, messiest, most meaningful professions on Earth.

One Last Thing

We take our work seriously, but we don't take ourselves too seriously. And neither should you. There are enough white papers and grim reports about the "future of luxury."

This isn't one of them.

This is a love letter.

To the marmalade on the breakfast tray.

To the porter who remembers the dog's name.

To the cracked ceramic bowl that somehow makes the soup taste better.

It's for those who still believe that intention beats trend, care beats concept and meaning outlasts marble.

So, welcome. The house is open. The light is warm. The stories are ready. You've made it to the lobby.

Let's begin.

CHAPTER ONE
Over-crowded

Part One
Four Over-Crowding Issues

Before we can imagine a better future for hospitality, we must confront some of the challenges of our current reality, starting with one of their most powerful symptoms: over-crowding. Across the globe, from city squares to cultural landmarks, the signs are everywhere. We'll look at some of the visible (and even invisible) consequences of over-crowding, from clogged landmarks and frustrated travellers, to deeper issues like gentrification and displacement, rising emissions and the erosion of local craft, knowledge and even authenticity.

What may seem like a nuisance is, in fact, a threat to the very future of travel. If left unchecked, over-crowding risks hollowing out the places that make hospitality meaningful, turning destinations into stage sets for influencers rather than living communities. For hoteliers, the question is not whether to act, but how. But paradoxically, while luxury travel has helped fuel this problem, it also holds part of the solution. High-end hotels may seem like passive beneficiaries of booming tourism, or even contributors to its pressures, but in reality, they are uniquely positioned to drive change, helping local areas retain their identity and making tourism more sustainable.

In the pages ahead, we'll explore both the forces driving over-crowding and the strategies that can re-anchor luxury hospitality in ways that preserve, rather than erode, the places it depends on. In doing so, we open the door to imagining a more responsible, place-sensitive hospitality.

Beautiful Places, Unsustainable Crowds

Tourism has grown exponentially in the last 50 years. In 1950 there were just 25 million international tourists. But by 2000 that number had increased to 600 million and reached a staggering 1.5 billion in 2024. Remarkably, it is set to reach 2.5 billion sometime after 2030. To put things in perspective, Portugal now has more tourists than the whole world did in 1950.

However, this dramatic growth isn't evenly distributed and luxury tourism has actually accelerated even faster, adding further complexity to the over-crowding dilemma, a change fuelled by the disproportionate increase in the High New worth (HNW) and Ultra High Net Worth (UHNW) population segments over the last few decades.

That might all seem like good news for hoteliers, but by the years leading up to 2018, travel professionals had begun to recognise the negative impacts of over-tourism, impacts that local residents had been warning about for much longer.

Of course, for many high-end travellers, there have always been too many tourists. No-one sees themselves as part of the problem. Even when Lord Byron, Mary and Percy Shelley visited Chamonix in the summer of 1814, they entered the Hôtel de Londres only to find it was overrun by English people and decided to move on.

Recently, in Rome, a friend had done his homework. "Arrive early," the travel blogs insisted, "Beat the queues if you don't already have a ticket." So, naturally, he turned up just before 7 a.m., only to discover that several thousand people had done exactly the same. The queue was already snaking along the Vatican's outer wall, a polite but determined mass of early risers, all armed with coffee cups and sun hats. By the time the gates opened, the line felt more like the start of a marathon than a pilgrimage. Inside, things moved briskly, if a little mechanically. The Raphael Rooms were beautiful, but it was more of a shuffle than a stroll. Stopping too long meant blocking the flow. "Keep moving," urged the security staff with the weary tone of people who've said it several hundred times already that morning.

The Sistine Chapel, when he reached it, was impressive, but crowded. A low murmur echoed around the room, occasionally broken by a firm "No photos, please, silencio!" followed by several flashes. It wasn't quite the hushed, awe-inspiring moment he'd imagined. Still, the ceiling was magnificent, when you could catch a clear view.

Outside, he rejoined the sunlight and paused for a coffee. A little less magical, perhaps, than he'd hoped for, but memorable nonetheless. Perhaps it has always been thus in Rome?

Historically, tourist destinations and countries have unsurprisingly aimed to attract as many tourists as possible, as the more tourists, the more revenue. Today tourist boards across the world continue to market their attractions. Attractions continue to set ever-higher visitor targets and countries celebrate record-breaking tourism numbers. But in too many places, the scales have tipped. The negative impacts now outweigh the positives for many stakeholders.

Take the Louvre: with nine million visitors in 2024, it announced plans for a dedicated Mona Lisa room to allow for a slightly more serene viewing experience. From 2028 it will require an extra ticket and additional queueing, assuming all goes according to plan.

Up to a certain level of crowding, everyone can enjoy themselves and achieve their personal objectives. But then we all hit a tipping point; not only do the latecomers suffer, but no one enjoys it any more. It's like traffic gridlock: one too many cars and everyone stands still.

Consider destinations that were not even on the tourism map just a few years ago. Take Iceland, suddenly overrun by tourists after a Justin Bieber video. Or the Faroe Islands, yes, the Faroes, whose government decided to close the country to visitors for a time after an influx of visitors, ironically searching for pristine places, threatened to overwhelm the islands' infrastructure.

CLOSED FOR MAINTENANCE, OPEN FOR VOLUNTOURISM

To address global overtourism, the Faroe Islands' Prime Minister famously announced the country was "closed for maintenance."

Instead of traditional tourists, volunteers were invited to build infrastructure alongside locals. The initiative went viral, attracting sign-ups from across the world within four days. By turning tourism into voluntourism, the Island's top ten sights have successfully been improved.

News Stories	Reach	SoMe Actions	Volunteers	PR ROI	Media Budget
511	3.720 million	34 million	3,500	120%	0

Source: Visit Faroe Islands 2019

Elsewhere we are all often horrified by images of Santorini's scenic spots overrun with influencers chasing the perfect sunset shot. But perhaps the most iconic image of over-tourism is that of mountaineers queuing on Everest's narrow summit ridge waiting their turn to finish the climb.

Arguably, for hoteliers, overtourism looks rather different. According to various projections, global tourism is expected to grow another 50% in the next 15 years. A rising number of people seeking accommodation and experiences presents numerous opportunities and suggests a very positive short to medium outlook. Between 2023 and 2025, at least 15 luxury hotels opened, or are soon to open, in London. Peninsula, Raffles, Six Senses, Waldorf Astoria and Park Hyatt all launched in the capital. Mandarin Oriental and Rosewood added to their existing portfolios. Similar trends are playing out in Paris, Milan, Rome and other major cities.

But the real problem is that overtourism isn't just about queues or strained infrastructure, it's that it slowly unravels the soul of a place. As ever-growing numbers of visitors descend upon the same destinations, the local fabric begins to fray. Residents adapt or leave, businesses reorient toward quick tourist profits and the genuine character that once made a place special is eroded, making tourism unsustainable in the long-term. This isn't just a story of footfall; it's a story of loss. And perhaps nowhere is that loss more visible than in those neighbourhoods once considered the heartbeat of a city.

Losing the Local and the Authentic

Airbnb was founded in 2008. It was, in many ways, an incredible idea. A California based start-up, run by a young CEO aiming to make global travel affordable, local and authentic, it took off like wildfire. So much so that in the space of 10 years, it shook the foundations of communities in every major city in Europe and beyond.

Perhaps this success shouldn't be that surprising; after all money can be earned faster from tourists who opt for short stays than from locals who must live on a budget. Once higher earnings become possible from rentals or shops, real estate and rental prices inevitably rise and the 'tourism economy' begins to clash with the 'local economy.' The effects on a city are often immediate, yet while global tech firms move at lightning speed, democratic administrations and city councils struggle to keep pace.

In all these cases small shifts, multiplied by millions of travellers, transform the character of entire neighbourhoods. For when tourism tips into overtourism, beloved places don't just become crowded; they become unrecognisable.

Take Montmartre in Paris for example. It is quaint, charming and full of life. It has great bakeries, pastry shops, bars, cafés and restaurants. The atmosphere is village-like because people know each other. Locals live in Montmartre. Tourists come and go. But then Airbnb arrived. Suddenly landlords realised they could make more money renting to tourists than to long-term residents. Flat prices and rents began to rise. New listings were snapped up by Airbnb entrepreneurs and the state even began offering tax incentives to Airbnb landlords. In some buildings, residents grew upset because of the traffic and the noise and perhaps more importantly because strangers were invading their personal spaces. They felt less safe. Local food shops saw clients come and go, never staying long enough to become regulars. Prices increased alongside the rents, further alienating the locals and small, independent shops could not afford to stay.

Within a couple of years, residents started to leave for other parts of Paris. High-margin branded stores, rarely used by locals, moved in: lingerie, glassware and fashion retailers, along with three separate imported chocolate brands, all clustered on the same street. Junk tourist shops also started to appear, t-shirts, industrial sweets, branded soaps, the usual. Essential shopping became more difficult for locals and the area lost much of the quaint, local charm that had made it attractive in the first place.

Over the last two decades Airbnb and other platforms have disrupted some of Europe's most beloved neighbourhoods. They have globalised their model, perhaps unaware (or indifferent) to the local damage it causes. Worst of all, they're in the process of killing the golden goose. For once the Airbnb 'economy' has weakened or destroyed the local community, the area is left as a tourist trap offering a standardised, globalised experience.

Local and authentic? No longer.

Local Hardships

In 2017, residents of several popular European destinations, including Barcelona, Venice and Palma de Mallorca took to the streets to protest. The movement returned even more forcefully in the summer of 2024, as citizens across Italy, Spain, the Netherlands and even Lapland demonstrated against the relentless rise in tourism.

In response, the mayors of Amsterdam, Barcelona, Berlin, Paris and other European cities asked the European Commission for tighter regulation of digital platforms like Airbnb. They cited the negative impact of unregulated short-term rentals, which in many places had drastically reduced the stock of affordable housing.

But housing affordability is just the tip of the iceberg.

In The Guardian, an elderly resident of Valencia shares her heartbreaking story. Once surrounded by neighbours she knew well, her building was a close-knit community; her social life, her safety net.

Now, at 84, she's the only local left. She feels too old to move and if anything were to happen, there's no one she could turn to for help. She misses the daily chats over coffee, the sense of connection with local storeowners, that comfortable sense of knowing her neighbours. When she ventures out to shop, she finds prices have soared. She waits in line behind tourists glued to their phones. On the way home, she must navigate the sidewalk carefully, dodging rented electric scooters and bikes flying by.

Is this really the best we can do for residents and is it any wonder that resentment towards tourists continues to grow?

Crowds Mean Carbon

And while the social fabric of these cities is fraying, the environmental costs of mass tourism are mounting just as quickly. The equation is simple: as travel grows, so too do emissions, from the journeys themselves to the energy consumed once guests arrive. To put things in perspective, consider this: a round trip between a northern and a southern European city adds approximately 440 kg of CO_2 or equivalent per passenger to the atmosphere.[1]

Now let's compare that to emissions on-site. Washing a full linen bedding set in a hotel room emits around 2 kg CO_2e, while the overall carbon footprint of a single night's stay in a European hotel averages 12 kg CO_2e per guest, according to Circular Ecology.[2]

In other countries, like in Taiwan, that figure rises significantly, up to 29 kg CO_2e per room night.[3]

The numbers make the consequences clear. But to truly grasp where this path leads, let's fast forward a few years. What could 2035 look like if we continue on this trajectory?

Paris 2035: The Price of Doing Nothing

Imagine this: it's 2035. Paris is still here, but something essential is missing. The city has hit its tourism growth targets. In fact, it's exceeded them. Visitor numbers have surged by another 50%, just as projected. On paper, it's a success. But walk the streets and the city tells a different story.

The sidewalks are choked with luggage wheels, selfie sticks and queues that stretch across the plazas. From the Eiffel Tower to the Louvre, from Sacré-Cœur to Shakespeare & Company, crowds press in as if the entire city has become an open-air amusement park. Locals dodge the congestion with quiet resentment. Some just don't bother any more; they've moved out.

In once iconic neighbourhoods like Le Marais, Saint-Germain-des-Prés and Montmartre, tourists now outnumber residents. The charm is gone. Independent cafés and family-run boutiques have vanished, replaced by chains selling macarons, scented candles, or Eiffel Tower hoodies. The "local experience" has become a carefully packaged simulation, at Parisian prices.

To maintain some semblance of order, new pedestrian traffic regulations have been introduced. Certain streets are now one-way for foot traffic. Crowd flow systems blink from digital kiosks. And in the most congested areas, access is restricted altogether, entry is granted by timed quotas, enforced by QR codes. It's efficient, even necessary. But it feels sterile and not particularly Parisian. Historic museums and churches remain open, but mostly as photo backdrops. Culture has been reduced to content.

Meanwhile, rents have spiralled out of control. Small businesses have been priced out. Only luxury brands, themed concept stores, or high-margin souvenir shops survive. What was once a city of intimacy, taste and intellect, now fights for attention on price, popularity and influencer visibility.

Even the luxury sector is feeling it. Upscale hotels, once proud havens of refinement, now compete for oversaturated guests in peak season. High turnover, short stays and transactional service define the guest experience. Staff face burnout and churn.

Recruiting talent is harder than ever. Commutes from the outskirts are long and working in the centre no longer feels aspirational.

And then there's the climate. Heatwaves linger longer each summer. Air conditioning is no longer a luxury, it's essential. Energy demand surges. Outdoor terraces sit empty during the hottest hours of the day. The city sweats and with it, its soul withers a little also.

Tourism hasn't collapsed. But it has eroded everything that made Paris desirable in the first place. It's no longer a refined destination. It's a product and increasingly, a cliché. Discerning travellers have noticed. They go elsewhere.

What remains is a hollowed-out version of Paris, efficient, crowded, Instagrammable… and utterly forgettable. Is this the future we want to build? This isn't a dystopian fantasy, it's a logical projection of "business as usual." If growth continues unchecked and the hospitality sector remains passive, this is where it leads. The lesson for hoteliers is clear: growth without stewardship is a slow slide into mediocrity. And when the magic fades, it's not just cities that suffer, it's the brands, the teams and the trust we've built with our guests. The soul of the destination is not a renewable resource. Once it's lost, no marketing campaign can bring it back.

Many once-great destinations have already suffered this fate: Phuket, Phi Phi Island, Boracay, Zell am See. Even Barcelona and Rome are teetering on the edge. More and more travellers say they won't go back.

So, what can we do as hoteliers? Is this challenge too big for us, or can we make a meaningful contribution to positive change? We believe the answer is clear, we can contribute, we must contribute and in fact, we are uniquely positioned to lead that shift.

Part Two
Building a Better Tourism: From Over-crowding to Enjoyment

If Paris 2035 shows us the cost of inaction, then Amsterdam offers a glimpse of another path, one where the industry can take responsibility and actively shape a better balance between visitors, residents and place.

In 2018, the Amsterdam Tourism Board, I amsterdam, reoriented its goals, shifting the focus from pure tourism promotion to destination management, with the aim of better control of visitor flows and spreading tourism more sustainably throughout the city. [4] Its new mission was clear: to improve the quality of life for both residents and tourists. The strategy included several key measures: limiting the growth of the visitor economy, reducing low-value tourism (such as stag parties and their associated disturbances), promoting lesser-known areas of the city and surrounding regions and working with entrepreneurial partners to enhance shared infrastructure and facilities.

To support these goals, the city also implemented a range of concrete steps: certain residential areas were excluded from short-term holiday rentals, busy streets were encouraged to maintain attractive storefronts rather than being overrun by souvenir shops and public spaces were improved through increased street cleaning, more bins and noise-control measures such as curfews on party boats. Amsterdam was in fact the first city to adopt a tourism strategy that genuinely considered all stakeholders, including residents. They called it "tourism that works for all."

The city developed a seven-point action plan: a set of recommendations from the City to the City. This approach has proven highly effective, largely because it was built on consensus. Reaching that point wasn't easy, but they began by listening to all concerned parties. It was a true co-creation effort, involving residents, entrepreneurs, cultural institutions and experts. Unfortunately, not every city is as forward-thinking, or as prepared, for a multi-stakeholder approach. Many tourist destinations lack either the knowledge or the practical know-how to initiate such change.

So, what can we hoteliers do?

Creating Coalitions with Meaningful Goals

As Amsterdam demonstrates, the next step is clear, hoteliers must not act alone, but rather join with residents, businesses and local leaders to create coalitions that make life better for everyone by managing over-crowding.

Taking stock is a good place to start: what local initiatives already exist? Has anyone gathered a "coalition of the willing," and what's on their agenda? Identifying all the stakeholders is also a strong first step, better still if you can align around a common goal.

It only takes one person to spark an initiative, a bit of stamina to keep it going and a growing circle of supporters to build momentum. The good news for hoteliers? Hotels are built for connection. The space is already there and you control it. So why not put it to use? Pick one compelling, manageable angle on over-crowding and start there. You'll be surprised by the energy it creates.

Take Guests Away from Overcrowded Places

Coalitions, however, don't just work at the level of policy or community initiatives, they can also begin with the everyday choices hotels make for their guests. One of the most powerful contributions hoteliers can offer is to redirect demand itself, designing experiences that ease the pressure on over-crowded sites while giving travellers, particularly those from Gen Z, something far richer in return.

Gen Z travellers, raised on social media, are starting to realise something important: the very phones and apps that promise connection may actually be getting in the way, glamorizing travel to the point where it disconnects them from the culture around them. Instead of immersing themselves, travellers often race to "consume" a destination as quickly as possible, pressured to do it all and prove they enjoyed every moment. The result? Visitors end up more stressed in Vienna or Rome than they are at home, fighting for reservations, battling crowds and leaving completely exhausted. But isn't travel meant to be about relaxation and discovery?

That's where we, as hoteliers, have a unique opportunity. Inspired by the slow travel movement, we can help guests reconnect with the true spirit of exploration.

That opportunity only becomes a reality when we translate the idea of slow travel into concrete offerings, experiences that shift guests from passive consumers into active participants. So, what experiences are we offering at our hotels? Do we have "No Over-Tourism, No Instagram" tours that are authentic, local and co-created with our teams and community partners? Do they guide guests away from the usual tourist paths? These are the kinds of offerings our teams would be proud to promote and guests would share naturally once they're home.

The opportunity now is to design new, seasonal experiences with our local partners, always staying one step ahead of the crowds and one step closer to what travel is really about.

Depth should be promoted over breadth. Seeing and understanding one thing well often leaves a deeper impression than rushing through a dozen sights. Travellers who engage with art, history, or locals return home saying, "I learned something new and feel better for it." Taking people on deeper dives can mean spreading out the burden of tourism on a place by moving people away from crowding just the main sites. It can also mean a better experience for everyone.

Life-seeing is replacing sight-seeing. Many people are just as interested in understanding the lives of locals as big famous sites. And yet, while every hotelier should know this and most agree that experiences matter more than things, most hotels haven't updated their value chain to deliver home-made experiences to their guests. Experience design and delivery for hotel guests is often outsourced to third-parties, including guides, so our guests' satisfaction during their time in the city depends on people we don't employ. But imagine if guides were part of the hotel team, heading the Experience department (yes, even in cities, not just in resorts!). A trusted, in-house guide could design rich guest experiences and interactions that would steer guests clear of (and alleviate pressure on) over-crowded sites. It would transform the quality of the guest experience in harmony with the hotel's ethos. This would not happen overnight as travel agents and then guests would need to trust hotels who first decide to integrate the full guest experience to make it seamless and 'low-crowded'.

Let us return to the Louvre. Most visitors make a beeline for da Vinci's Mona Lisa, only to find themselves in a sea of smartphones, straining for a glimpse. Just a few steps away, however, hangs another da Vinci masterpiece: Saint John the Baptist. It's equally profound, yet quietly overlooked. There, guests can linger in a calm, almost private moment with a work of genius.

Imagine if this logic were taken even further: what if each painting in a gallery were curated as a stepping-stone, teaching you about a different aspect of painting, so that by the time the visitors get to the Mona Lisa, they're better able to truly appreciate it? It's in these overlooked moments that hotels can play a curatorial role, gently steering guests away from the expected and toward what's quietly extraordinary. This pattern isn't limited to museums. Across Paris, some of the greatest monuments hide in plain sight, overshadowed by fame but waiting to be rediscovered.

Helping guests unlock these hidden treasures takes more than a guidebook. It requires insider knowledge of the Louvre, a feel for art and an understanding of each guest's curiosity and pace. Most of all, it begins with real conversation, something that only happens when guides are part of the hotel experience and its team, not just outsourced for the day.

And when that kind of insider knowledge is paired with the willingness to guide guests beyond the obvious landmarks, an entirely different city begins to reveal itself. While millions visit Notre-Dame, few wander into Saint-Eustache, the city's second-largest church. Inside, masterpieces by Rubens, Vouet and Manetti wait quietly for those willing to stray just a little off the beaten path. Will your guests trust your team to lead them to these deeper, more personal discoveries? A hotel-employed guide, or dedicated "experience expert", can open doors that typical tours simply can't: a chat with a neighbourhood artisan, a moment with a local legend, or a subtle cultural nuance that becomes a lifelong memory. Indeed, hotels can also work with locals to do so much of what we've described above, from helping people explore the local lifestyle, to taking them on cycle rides around the city. This helps both the hotel guests, the hotel itself and of course the community that made the place iconic in the first place. These aren't just alternatives to the crowds. They're antidotes to over-tourism and far more meaningful experiences in their own right.

Control Social Media, Don't Suffer in Silence

Yet shaping where guests go is only half the task; the other half is shaping how they experience those places, free from the distorting lens of social media. By now, we all understand the benefits of social media and we're equally aware of how disruptive it can be. To some degree, most of us are addicted. Hotel marketing teams constantly chase more posts, more likes, more visibility. But in the process, they may be unintentionally fuelling the very problems we're trying to solve. The dream of every marketing assistant is to go viral, yet the irony is that viral fame often destroys the very magic it seeks to promote. It funnels crowds to the same places, at the same time, diluting the uniqueness of the experience. Instant Instagram or TikTok fame may bring a brief spotlight, but at a long-term cost.

Fundamentally, when guests spend more time curating content than being present, they unintentionally turn meaningful travel into something shallow and performative. But when they spend more time socially and less time posting, they start to break the cycle of funnelling tourists to the same over-promoted destinations, helping preserve the authenticity and balance of the places they visit.

It may seem bold, but a thoughtful, hotel-wide social media policy can actually enhance the guest experience, helping travellers reconnect with the moment and with the place. As travel professionals, we know what can spoil a great experience. And while it may seem like the tide is too strong to resist, some hotels and private clubs have already taken meaningful steps. The result? Guests, though initially surprised, often end up appreciating and even applauding, the change. Some areas of hotels could be designated as social media–free zones. No-photo policies are becoming more common, particularly in dining rooms. Even "no-internet" zones are emerging. While this may sound radical, guest feedback has been overwhelmingly positive, especially when alternative Wi-Fi areas are clearly provided nearby.

A simple solution could also be to divide public areas into two distinct categories: Social Spaces and Screen Spaces. After all, meaningful human connection and screen time rarely coexist. Social Spaces could be intentionally Wi-Fi free, encouraging real interaction, while Screen Spaces allow guests to scroll, post and recharge online. This subtle separation not only improves the atmosphere but also makes guests more conscious of their screen habits. When Wi-Fi isn't always-on everywhere, it naturally creates moments of awareness and invites guests to reflect on how they're engaging with their surroundings. This isn't about rejecting technology. It's about reclaiming presence and helping guests rediscover a more grounded, more enriching way to travel. The hotel industry cannot effect this change on its own, but it can do its part to help travellers become aware of more conscious ways to travel.

Part 3
Preserving the Local and the Authentic

For seasoned travellers, there's little reason to explore the world unless the experience offers something truly local and authentic. It's a concept the travel industry frequently champions, but one that's becoming harder to find in a globalised world. Across Europe and beyond, local factories and small workshops have moved offshore. Independent businesses are being pushed out by international chains that now dominate main streets. Luxury brands seek to occupy every prime retail location. The balance between global and local is shifting fast, leaving many cities feeling less unique than they did just a few years ago. There's also a deeper demographic shift at play. In ageing economies like those of Europe and Japan (and indeed, even countries like Tunisia and Vietnam), local workers are in short supply. Fewer people are entering service, craft, or manual trades, roles essential to preserving local character. The service may be excellent, but the local flavour is missing. When international brands move in with entirely different value chains, small local businesses can't compete and are often priced out of city centres altogether. The problem is clear: international chains are not local. They rarely sell locally made products and often don't hire from the local community. That's a far cry from the "local and authentic" experience guests are increasingly seeking. And of course, international chains are also not part of a circular economy either; as profits go to other countries and communities. What travellers truly want are distinctive, homegrown brands; products crafted nearby; and services delivered by local people who are truly part of the place. The challenge is preserving that authenticity and finding practical ways to support it, before it disappears entirely.

How Can We Hoteliers Help?

This erosion of local character isn't just an aesthetic loss, it undermines the very ecosystems that give places their vitality, making it all the more urgent for hotels to step in as anchors that protect, support and amplify what remains. Part of the solution is making hotels community anchors, powerful nodes for collaboration within networks of local people, businesses and institutions. But to make this a reality we first need to ask ourselves: How do we define our hotel's Direct Zone of Influence (DZI)?

For many, the DZI (a term often used in studies of architecture and infrastructure) might be limited to the hotel building and the pavement in front. But if we're serious about promoting what's local and authentic, that definition must stretch further, to encompass the surrounding neighbourhood, quartier, barrio, or Nachbarschaft. How that neighbourhood looks, feels and functions has a direct impact on your hotel's success and your hotel has an impact on it in return.

Hotels are often among the most prominent institutions in a community. They have visibility, foot traffic, dedicated teams and physical spaces, resources that could be leveraged to strengthen the local ecosystem in meaningful, lasting ways. This kind of engagement is more intimate, more relational. And the deeper the connection, the more resilient and vibrant the community becomes.

Hotels Have Spaces and the Means to Communicate

To turn influence into impact, hotels can use what they already possess, space, staff and communication platforms that can make them natural anchors of community life. Some hotels already do more than welcome travellers. They serve as hubs for local connection, creativity and communication. Take the Eaton Hotel in Washington, DC. It operates its own radio station and video studio, offering a platform for local voices and ideas. It not only strengthens ties within the community but also gives guests a richer, more authentic experience of place. Some hotels even publish local newsletters or newspapers, giving a voice to people and projects that might otherwise go unnoticed. Who else in the neighbourhood has a full team of PR and marketing professionals, ready-made event spaces and an internal communications infrastructure? Hotels do. That's a powerful position from which to support local culture and connection.

While hotels have unique assets to share, they're not alone; other institutions can also show what this kind of rooted, multi-layered community engagement looks like. An inspiring example comes from the Saint-Eustache church in central Paris, near Les Halles, the city's historic food market. At one end of the cultural spectrum, it partners with the Bourse de Commerce, a major contemporary art museum funded by François Pinault. The museum lends modern artworks to the church, where they're shown alongside Rubens and Manetti. At the other end, Saint-Eustache runs a nightly soup kitchen at 6 p.m., feeding those in need. The sense of community is so strong that there are often more volunteers than roles to fill. Recently, the church also teamed up with Greta Metehor School of Guides to offer free English-language tours of the site, opening its history to a wider audience.

The goodwill generated through such initiatives is immense. Volunteers feel they're doing something meaningful. They see the results close to home, in their own neighbourhood. And the community becomes stronger, more connected and more alive as a result.

Eating and Drinking: A True Test of Local and Authentic

Food and drink consistently top travellers' must-do lists. But what does "local and authentic" really feel like when it comes to restaurants and cafés?

Consider the contrast:

There are a number of internationally celebrated French pastry chefs in London, all with global followings running into millions. At their various outlets in some of London's top hotels, a coffee and a patisserie costs over £22, while their afternoon teas can be found for more than £85. Just as their work spans continents, so too do their clientele which is predominantly international. Locals at these cafés are few and far between, and you could be anywhere in the world.

Now compare that to Elysée Saint Honoré, a Brasserie on Avenue Hoche, just down the road from the elegant Raffles Royal Monceau in Paris. Sit at the counter, order a coffee and a tartine, a baguette with delicious jam and watch the daily ballet of life unfold: sanitation workers, delivery drivers, suited professionals and tourists, all popping in for their morning fix. Listen to the banter and local gossip exchanged over the bar. The bill? €3.80. If you sit down in the restaurant section, it costs a bit more. But the sense of place? Priceless.

There are grades of local feel in hospitality. A venue isn't "local" if most of its customers aren't local. Community happens when regulars know each other and share conversations, when staff notice who's missing or ask after someone's exam results or family member's health. That's what creates the "village atmosphere" everyone remembers.

For hoteliers, the opportunity lies in making locals into regulars and making hotel regulars feel like locals. Let the guests themselves generate a warm, genuine sense of community and authenticity.

Bringing it Back to the Hotel: Curating Local Tours from Within

Just as Saint-Eustache shows how cultural institutions can weave themselves into the fabric of their neighbourhood, hotels too can play this role, by curating experiences that begin within their own walls. It starts by asking the questions, what truly local, authentic tours does your hotel offer? Were they imagined by your own team and are they led by them? These questions are vital because a well-crafted tour does more than showcase a destination. It connects guests with your staff, your neighbourhood and the people who give the place its soul. These experiences might include visits to lesser-known cultural sites, independent boutiques, neighbourhood cafés, or local markets. Guests might meet artists in their studios, or even share a conversation over tea in someone's home. The potential for joy and for creating unforgettable memories, is enormous. And when guests return to the hotel, the experience doesn't end. Those moments carry on in conversations, between guests, team members and even the locals they met along the way. The hotel becomes a place where stories are exchanged, not just rooms are booked. The lesson? Authentic local experiences don't have to stay outside the hotel. When curated with care, they can start and grow, right from within.

Demographics and Meaningful Work: A New Frontier

If tours and cultural experiences can connect guests more deeply to place, then hiring and working with locals offers the same opportunity, rooting the hotel itself in the life of its neighbourhood. But as many of us have experienced, hiring local staff in Europe is already a challenge and demographic shifts over the coming decades will only make it more difficult. Yet at the same time, we know that today's jobseekers increasingly value purpose, as "doing meaningful work" consistently ranks among their top three priorities. And many people feel a strong connection to their neighbourhood and want to contribute to its well-being.

A hotel that actively collaborates with its local community and serves the common good becomes more than a workplace. Like Saint-Eustache in Paris, it becomes a magnet, drawing people in, not just for what it offers, but for what it stands for.

People want to be part of something meaningful.

The opportunity is clear: by leveraging the resources they already possess, such as spaces, teams, expertise and visibility, hotels can effect real change, strengthening communities, amplifying local voices and supporting initiatives that leave a lasting, positive mark close to home.

Part Four
Levers and Solutions to Minimise the Impact on Local Communitites

We've explored the importance of preserving what's local and authentic and the potential role hotels can play in revitalizing their neighbourhoods. Now the question becomes: how can hoteliers measure and understand the true state of the neighbourhoods they depend on?

A healthy neighbourhood is essential, not only for residents, but for the long-term success of the hotel itself. With this expanded definition of the hotel's zone of influence, properties can and should, act as credible voices in conversations with local authorities. In many cases, hotels are central players in their communities, with more leverage and visibility than any single resident or small business.

The actions discussed earlier can go a long way. However, to be truly effective, efforts should be tied to clear goals and those goals start with a solid understanding of what's happening in the neighbourhood. What affects the locals today? What pressures are they facing? The first step: conduct a neighbourhood health diagnostic.

This diagnostic, created in collaboration with local stakeholders, offers a snapshot of the community's current well-being. A radar chart can help visualise the key dimensions to monitor, such as social, physical, mental, spiritual and economic health.

This may feel outside a hotelier's usual comfort zone, so let's bring it to life with two real-world examples, from Freiburg, Germany and Copenhagen, Denmark.

Freiburg: The City That Feels Good To Be In

With a group of inspiring people, we spent five days in Freiburg, exploring eco-design and sustainability in action. The city has already developed such a sophisticated response to sustainability that simply being there feels transformative, not just for those passionate about the planet, but for anyone seeking a better way of living. At the end of our stay, one participant summed it up perfectly:

"It's incredible, everyone in Freiburg seems happy. And it rubs off on us."

That happiness isn't accidental. It's the product of a model of sustainability that goes beyond buildings and transport systems. In Freiburg, sustainability is social: it's about belonging, inclusion and the daily practices that make a community thrive. The result of a collective effort by Freiburg's citizens to create a liveable, inclusive and genuinely sustainable city During our time in Freiburg we met Daniela, the community manager of the Rieselfeld neighbourhood. Trained in social inclusion, she's launched multiple initiatives: a community café, weekly dance nights and gathering spaces where neighbours connect, laugh and build friendships. Residents count down the days to Dance Night, it's the highlight of their week. We also met Rosa, a volunteer who manages community relations in a large apartment complex. She knew everyone's name, their stories, their lives. For Rosa, it wasn't about property or square meters, it was about human connection. And because of her, people didn't just live there. They loved living there.

Freiburg is full of people like Daniela and Rosa, whose small, meaningful actions create a sense of welcome that lingers long after you leave. Imagine the impact if your guests, your team and your community felt the same.

Scenario:	**A Morning in Freiburg**
Setting:	A bright, sunlit community café in Rieselfeld, Freiburg. The smell of fresh pastries and coffee fills the air. International hoteliers gather at a long wooden table, curious and attentive. Soft music plays in the background, blending with the sound of laughter and the clinking of coffee cups. Daniela, the neighbourhood's community manager, steps forward with a warm smile.

Characters:	
Daniela:	The neighbourhood's community manager
Sophie:	A bright and curious hotelier from Paris
Marco:	A hotelier from Milan just starting to think about this problem
Rosa:	A volunteer who manages community relations in a large apartment complex

---

Daniela:	Welcome to Rieselfeld! I'm so glad you're here. We don't often host hoteliers, but honestly, we probably should. You're in the business of hospitality, just like us, only we do it more at a neighbourhood level.
Sophie:	Thanks, Daniela. We've heard a lot about Freiburg's community spirit, what part do you guys play in nurturing that and how does your role fit into that process?
Daniela:	*(Grinning)* My role? Well, essentially I try to make it easier for strangers to become neighbours. So, that means not only hosting a whole range of events, but also listening to people's problems, noticing what's happening in the community and trying to nudge people to help out too. The aim is to basically create the kind of spaces where once they show up once, they want to come back. Not because they have to, but because it feels good just to hang out there, right?
Marco:	But people are always so busy, do they really have time to just drop by?
Daniela:	Honestly, people just crave a real, low-pres-

sure time and space to hang out with old friends and even to make connections with new ones.

A woman walks in, waves cheerfully. Daniela lights up.

Daniela: Speaking of old friends, this is Rosa, one of our community volunteers. She's really the soul of her building and the reason so many of the residents know each other now.

Marco: Daniela told us you know everyone in your building. Really?

Rosa: Not to blow my own trumpet, but yes, basically. I suppose it's because I do the things I think are important, or what I'd want people to do for me. I stop by with soup, try to remember birthdays, organise potlucks, that sort of thing. It's essential, because I think that when people trust their neighbours, they become more open and slowly, they also start doing this kind of thing for others too. They feel like they belong.

Daniela: Right, right, we often say: belonging before branding. Basically, real well-being doesn't come from perfect lighting or like the most polished design. It comes from how people are welcomed, how they're listened to, or how they're treated.

Marco: I suppose the challenge is that in hotels, guests come and go, which makes it harder to build that sense of belonging in a much shorter time.

Daniela: I hear that, but I do think it's possible. I think the focus has got to be… something around… thinking beyond the stay. So inviting locals in, co-hosting events with artists, schools, or food producers. Or even stuff like creating chances for guests to meet just normal people within the community and for the community to meet itself.

Eva: This all makes it sound doable. Although a lot of hard work!

Rosa: *(Smiling)*
You don't need to reinvent hospitality. Just humanize it. And when in doubt? Ask yourself: What would make me feel welcome here? And then offer exactly that.

Copenhagen: Designing Spaces That Build Belonging

Further north, in the heart of Christianhavn, Copenhagen, stands Kanalhuset, a hotel born from a belief in the power of community. Its founders, Lennart and Suzanne Lajboschitz, (creators of the popular retail brand Flying Tiger), started their community journey by purchasing a decommissioned church in the less than trendy Vesterbro district. They transformed it into Folkehuset Absalon, a community house where neighbours gather for everything from art classes and yoga to dance parties and communal dinners.

Absalon feels like an extension of one's living room, warm, playful and full of energy. But what binds it all together is the belief that social bonds make life meaningful and that these bonds need physical, welcoming spaces to grow. With around 60 events per week, Absalon thrives. But its most important tradition is the daily social dinner. Long tables are set. Phones and social media are not allowed. The only other rule: talk to your neighbour. The concept was so successful that the couple decided to bring it to hospitality. After opening a hotel on the Danish coast, they launched Kanalhuset, on a quiet canal street in Christianhavn. The hotel is packed most nights. So is dinner.

At 7 p.m. sharp, friends and strangers sit side by side, just like at Absalon. Conversation flows. The buzz spills into the bar and often picks back up again over breakfast after morning yoga.

The World Happiness Report 2025, from Oxford University's Wellbeing Research Centre, listed shared meals as one of the seven most effective ways to increase happiness. Kanalhuset shows why: it fosters connection, warmth and a real sense of belonging.

What Can We Learn From Freiburg and Copenhagen?

These stories aren't about grand gestures. They're about creating spaces where relationships form naturally, where people feel seen, heard and connected. What this tells us is that at their best, a hotel can:

- Serve as the heart of a neighbourhood.
- Build or support initiatives that strengthen community health.
- Host events and engage with local actors.
- Define its success not only by occupancy rates, but by its contribution to neighbourhood well-being.

And when our hotels become meaningful to the communities that surround them, they become magnets, bringing together staff, guests and partners alike.

So, let's not underestimate the ripple effect of small, local actions. They just might make someone want to stay that little bit longer and even return often.

Part Five
Levers to Reduce Emissions Caused by Over-Crowding

If Freiburg and Copenhagen show us the power of small, local actions to strengthen communities, the next step is to recognise that those same principles apply on a global scale, where the challenge is not only social connection but also the environmental impact of over-crowding.

Thierry Marx, the multi–Michelin-starred chef, social activist and now head of France's national hospitality association (UMIH), recently made a striking comment:

> *"When you buy a baguette at €0.80 in a supermarket (versus €1.20 in a bakery), you're actually paying for it three times, at the checkout, with your health and in environmental damage."*

Sadly, the same logic applies to those irresistible €19.99 low-cost flights across Europe. They may be cheap on paper, but they don't reflect the real cost: the environmental toll of flying, PR strain of over-tourism and the growing pressure on local communities. Like the supermarket baguette, the true price is simply deferred, externalised and paid elsewhere. The irony is hard to miss: these quick, low-cost getaways are sold as escapes from the stresses of everyday life, yet they end up contributing to more emissions, more crowds and ultimately more stress.

But there are alternatives, models that offer the same freedom but without the side effects and some of them are already reshaping how people travel, nudging them toward slower, more conscious behaviours.

Consider, for example, Deutsche Bahn's €58 regional pass, launched as a trial in summer 2023 and now a permanent offer. For the price of two short-haul flights, it gives passengers unlimited access to slower, quieter travel across Germany for an entire month. It's affordable, climate-conscious and encourages a different kind of journey, one that lingers, digresses and often leads to hidden gems surprisingly close to home.

Three Avenues Worth Exploring

By now, the message is clear, encouraging longer stays and reducing ultra-short breaks benefits almost everyone, except, perhaps, ultra-low-cost airlines. Here's the simple math: two 3-night trips instead of three 2-night trips means one fewer flight, a 33% reduction. Considering that flights can account for up to 85% of a trip's total CO_2e emissions, that's a very significant reduction.

But this is more than just a math problem, it's a structural one. According to Eurostat, in 2023, 56% of trips by EU residents lasted between 1 and 3 nights. This trend is driven largely by the availability of cheap, frequent flights that make quick getaways seem irresistible. However, here's the catch, there are short breaks and then there are ultra-short breaks, the 1- or 2-night stays that barely allow time to connect with a place. And they're often the real problem. Ultra-short breaks are the tourism equivalent of ultra-fast fashion or food porn, built for instant gratification, heavy on impact and light on substance. And while they may look good in a feed, they leave behind a trail of environmental and cultural destruction. It's worth noting that ultra-fast fashion is already under investigation by regulators in the US, France and beyond for its social and ecological harms, so perhaps ultra-fast tourism is not so far behind?

The writing is on the wall. With growing momentum behind sustainable travel, it's easy to imagine regulators turning their attention to companies that promote and profit from ultra-short breaks. So the question isn't if scrutiny is coming, but whether we'll wait for it, or lead the way.

To truly tackle the challenge, we need to understand Gen Z, the first generation to grow up entirely online and now the most active segment of short- and ultra-short-break travellers.

Enter Gen Z: The Paradox of Freedom and Frequency

Among today's travellers, Gen Z stands out as the most active adopters of short and ultra-short city breaks. Armed with budget-friendly platforms, social media inspiration and an appetite for spontaneous experiences, Gen Z is reshaping tourism across Europe. City breaks, trips lasting one to three nights, are their most favoured form of travel. Many take multiple such trips each year, often hopping between destinations for the price of a dinner out. It's travel as a series of quick hits, short on time, light on planning, heavy on content creation.

But here's where it gets interesting. This behaviour presents a striking paradox. Gen Z is also the first generation to fully embrace remote and flexible work, a shift that opens the door to longer, slower and more sustainable travel. With fewer constraints on time and place, they are uniquely positioned to take fewer trips, stay longer and integrate more deeply with local communities, exactly the kind of travel that reduces emissions and supports more balanced tourism. And yet that's not what's happening.

Instead, the convenience of cheap flights, paired with the pressure to "see more" and post often, is encouraging more frequent, shorter trips, ironically, the most carbon-intensive way to travel. The potential of remote work to reduce travel frequency is being undermined by the ease of booking and the social appeal of constant movement. Gen Z is travelling more, not less, despite having the tools to travel better.

This disconnect is more than generational. It reflects a broader tension in modern tourism: between the possibility of meaningful, sustainable experiences and the reality of convenience-driven, high-turnover travel. The challenge now is to help shift the narrative, from fast, fleeting escapes to slower, more rooted journeys that align with both the values and opportunities of a new era of travel.

What Can Hoteliers Do?

This paradox places hoteliers in a unique position. On one side, Gen Z has the freedom and tools to embrace slower, more sustainable travel; on the other, convenience and social media keep driving them toward frequent, short, high-impact trips. Hotels sit right in the middle of this tension, with a rare ability to influence which way the balance tips.

So, let's start with a few honest questions. Do you believe sustainability is more than a buzzword? Do you see how climate change is already shaping your guests' expectations and experiences? And do you agree that the problem will only worsen if nothing changes?

If the answer is yes, even a tentative yes, then the opportunity is clear. Hotels can discourage ultra-short trips and encourage longer, slower, more rooted stays. Three nights or more can become the new benchmark for meaningful travel. And this shift isn't just good for the planet. Longer stays also mean richer guest experiences, stronger local ties and more resilient business.

So how do we make that shift real? It doesn't start with grand gestures, but with the everyday choices that shape a stay, from how we set prices, to how we frame travel decisions, to how we design the guest experience once they arrive.

Exploring Options

Reducing emissions isn't just about grand gestures. It often starts with the way we shape a stay, from pricing to strategy. There are three promising avenues worth exploring, each pointing to a more thoughtful model of hospitality.

First: Pricing Strategy

Pricing is one of the most powerful tools in the hotelier's hands. Yet, most of the time, it's used purely to respond to demand. What if it could do more? What if pricing encouraged holidays rather than rushed, carbon-intensive breaks? By gently nudging guests toward longer stays, we could reduce the number of short-haul flights they book and by extension, their footprint.

In fact, some hotels have already begun to introduce a meaningful CO_2 charge for leisure stays of one or two nights. The fee isn't just symbolic; it feeds into a hotel-grown scheme to help compensate for the environmental impact of that brief trip, scaled appropriately to the length of stay. The aim isn't to shame guests, but to raise awareness and offer tangible solutions.

And let's not whisper about this either. Hotels committed to climate resilience can and should, make a song and dance about short breaks. The point is not to grandstand, but to be honest about the cost of a culture built around quick, cheap getaways. It's not about guilt, it's about clarity.

Second: A Guest-Friendly Approach to Reducing Local Emissions

While pricing strategies are important, coercion alone rarely changes behaviour. The stick must come with a carrot. The traditional "four nights for the price of three" offer has been around forever, but it rarely sets hearts racing. A fourth night in a city isn't always what guests want, unless that time is made more meaningful.

This is where conversation matters. Imagine simply asking at the point of inquiry: "How are you planning to travel here? Can we help you avoid the plane and the hassle?" Framed right, this doesn't come off as intrusive. It feels like a thoughtful concierge anticipating needs, exactly as great hoteliers always have.

By doing so, the hotel begins to take real ownership of Scope 3 emissions, those generated not within the hotel itself, but by its guests' travel and activity. That's a bold but necessary shift. Transport, after all, often accounts for most of a trip's emissions.

Third: A Local Emissions Strategy

Once on site, hotels can help reduce the local footprint too. Many already offer bikes, but availability isn't the same as use. What happens when a hotel actually tracks bike usage per guest, sets a target and aligns decisions with that goal? Suddenly, it's not just about offering the option, it's about creating the conditions for behaviour to shift. Collecting that data isn't just operational, it's strategic.

Think, too, about transfers. Is there a low-impact, comfortable, even luxurious way to travel from the train station to the hotel? Is the fleet electric? Are there agreements with local cab companies to prioritise EVs for hotel guests? Can guests text or tap to request one?

These small systems add up and they bring purpose back into roles that risk being diminished in a tech-driven world. In an era when AI can book a dinner or confirm a room upgrade, how does a concierge add value? Certainly, one way is by being a sustainability guide, someone who helps guests navigate the city in a way that's aligned with both their comfort and their conscience.

Ultimately, what begins with pricing, travel choices and local transport ends with something larger: a rebalancing of tourism itself. Tackling both over-crowding and emissions is not about fewer travellers, but about shaping how and where they travel.

Conclusion: Small Actions, Big Impact

Overcrowding isn't a distant threat. It's here, reshaping cities, distorting local life and placing increasing pressure on both communities and the climate. And for our industry the consequences are already visible: rising resentment, declining authenticity and a growing sense that even luxury is being commodified.

But this future is not inevitable. If today's trends continue, many beloved destinations may lose what made them desirable in the first place. But, if hospitality professionals, especially hoteliers, step into their full role as place-makers and partners, this trajectory can still be changed. Because here's the truth: we hoteliers hold more cards than we think. We are one of the few actors in the ecosystem with both visibility and resources, with the power to influence not just the guest experience, but the future of our neighbourhoods. We have teams, event spaces, communications tools and, most importantly, relationships with travellers who trust us.

But this isn't something one hotel can solve alone. It takes stakeholder collaboration, working alongside local artisans, cultural venues, guides, schools, city planners, transport operators and residents. Perhaps more importantly, it takes a shared project, one rooted in a real understanding of what makes your destination unique and what might help protect it. This new reality reshapes the job description of the hotel general manager. No longer just an operations, marketing, finance expert or brand ambassador, the GM becomes a community strategist, a convener of local voices, a steward of place. Success is no longer defined only by RevPAR, occupancy, or online ratings, but by the hotel's role in supporting a vibrant, liveable and authentic destination.

This is not just about sustainability. It's about strategy. A healthy, resilient and rooted local ecosystem isn't a "nice to have." It's the foundation of long-term success in high-end hospitality.

So, the question isn't whether change is needed.

The question is: who will lead it?

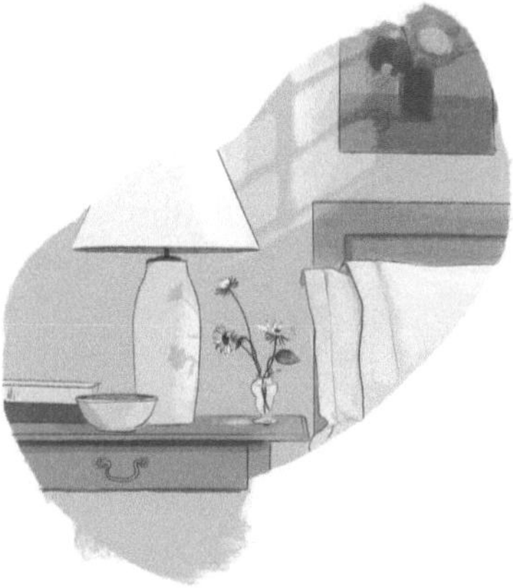

CHAPTER TWO

Under-staffed

Part One
Four Over-Crowding Issues

Today, the luxury hospitality sector is booming. Many luxury hotel groups are expanding at an unprecedented rate, adding properties across the globe and setting exponential targets for themselves.

Growth appears unstoppable.

On the surface, all appears to be well with our world. And yet, with the huge changes in societal demographics that are occurring, our sector, like many others, is facing a series of almost unprecedented challenges as we try to do more with less people. These challenges are myriad, with rising costs, inconsistent service delivery and an alarming shortage of skilled talent converging to create a multilayered crisis. We are trying to deliver more, to more people, with fewer and fewer hands. What once felt like a temporary staffing challenge is now a systemic problem and one that threatens not just our operations, but the very soul of what makes hospitality luxurious.

This chapter explores the roots of the labour crisis and challenges hoteliers to confront a hard truth; that hospitality has unintentionally undermined its own talent pipeline through decades of centralisation, outsourcing and underinvestment. We question why traditional recruitment no longer really works, how the meaning of work is shifting for many young people and how amidst these challenges, we can not only survive but thrive. Ultimately, instead of asking "where are the workers?", we must challenge ourselves to ask, "what kind of work and workplaces, are we offering?" Only then can we build a future where hospitality remains a career not only worth choosing, but staying in.

It is tempting to think that this isn't our problem as business owners, that it belongs to politics or society at large. But in truth, it is our problem too, because every business ultimately depends on the same pool of human resources. Although most businesses mainly take the best people they can get; they don't think about the problem of where those people are coming from or the other effects this has on the economy. But in an ideal world, businesses don't just take in talent, they also create it; they create a different kind of "circular" economy that doesn't drain the pool of talent but instead grows and develops it.

Ideally, of course, governments would help with this huge task and sometimes they do. But it's an enormous problem and probably unfixable without the work of those in the industry itself, who, in many cases, know better than anyone what needs to be done. Furthermore, we now live in such a globalised time that no one government is ever going to be fully responsible for the whole problem of the service economy. So now is the time where we all must step into leadership and help with these huge, pressing issues. For it is only by offering education, by sharing what we love, that we can help those we work with to focus their attention on the things that matter most.

Four Understaffing Challenges:

Before we can discuss solutions, let us lay out the key problems the sector faces. As we see it these can be split up into four key challenges:

1. The inability to deliver for guests due to a lack of potential staff available in the market
2. The inability to deliver quality to guests because of culture, skills and behaviour gaps
3. The inability to deliver this quality consistently to guests
4. The rising cost of HR and delivery

These challenges, shrinking labour supply, skills gaps, inconsistency in delivery and rising costs, are converging into a crisis that threatens the very essence of luxury hospitality. The first and most urgent of these challenges is the labour market itself, where shrinking supply makes even basic recruitment a daily struggle.

Part Two The Labour Market Challenge

Recruitment Questions

Can I recruit enough staff to run my property? Is anyone still looking for a job in hospitality? And if they are, will they choose to work for me? Will I find the right people, with the right education and training? And if I do recruit them, will they actually stay? Such questions are on the mind of every hotelier today. The fear is simple: if these challenges aren't solved, we won't be able to deliver for our guests. But why is this such a struggle in Europe and other developed countries?

Demographics x Overtourism

As we discussed in chapter one, the sector faces a significant overtourism problem, driven by an exponential growth in international visitor numbers. For recruitment, this presents a huge challenge as it requires an equally rapid growth in employees. While this may be good news in some parts of the world, in Europe and other ageing economies, it comes at precisely the wrong time, just as demographic trends are making this kind of recruitment almost impossible. The case of the Savoy in London presents a microcosm of these challenges. There the renowned Head Chef Anton Edelmann once led a kitchen of 120 chefs. The pace was relentless. The Savoy's reputation and Edelmann's own, was so strong that young chefs would queue for a chance to work there. But in 1998, something shifted. He interviewed a young man who, after the interview, said he had several offers to consider and would "think about it." Edelmann was stunned. Unbeknownst to him, the tide had turned. Until then, around 90% of his kitchen staff had come from across the European Union. But the EU had begun to tip into demographic decline. Fewer 18- to 25-year-olds were entering the workforce and fewer still were seeking jobs in hospitality. Every year since, those numbers have continued to drop.

Since the origins of tourism in the 18th century, with the rise of the Grand Tour, there has been a steady, reliable supply of labour eager to work in hotels. But now for the first time in history, across Europe, that supply is shrinking. Yet just when we need more people in hospitality than ever before, the labour pool is shrinking sharply, creating complex challenges that reverberate across every sector, including our own.

An Ageing Workforce

This shortage of local workers is already a serious issue in Europe, Japan, Korea and other ageing economies and it will become even more acute over the next 20 years. Every year, we need more people in the hospitality workforce, yet fewer are entering the job market. The result, millions fewer people under the age of 50 available to work, while the number of elderly citizens continues to rise rapidly. The graph below starkly illustrates this demographic shift between 2007 and 2022 and the next 15 years are projected to be even more dramatic.

POPULATION PYRAMIDS EU 2007 & 2022

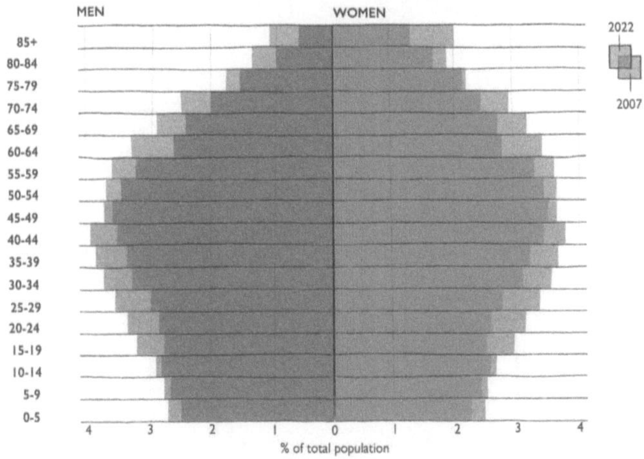

Source: Eurostat, "Population by age and sex, and population projections" EUROPOP2023

Take the relationship between the UK and Italy as an example. In 1962, Italy recorded nearly one million births. Around the same time, the UK relaxed its immigration laws, allowing Italians to enter the country. Italians quickly filled most service positions and came to dominate London's restaurants and bars.

For more than sixty years, Italian managers formed the backbone of many of London's top restaurants and bars. By 2022, however, this model had begun to unravel. Even well-regarded venues struggled to recruit and retain staff, exposing a growing vulnerability in the UK hospitality sector.

This illustrates the perfect storm facing UK hospitality:

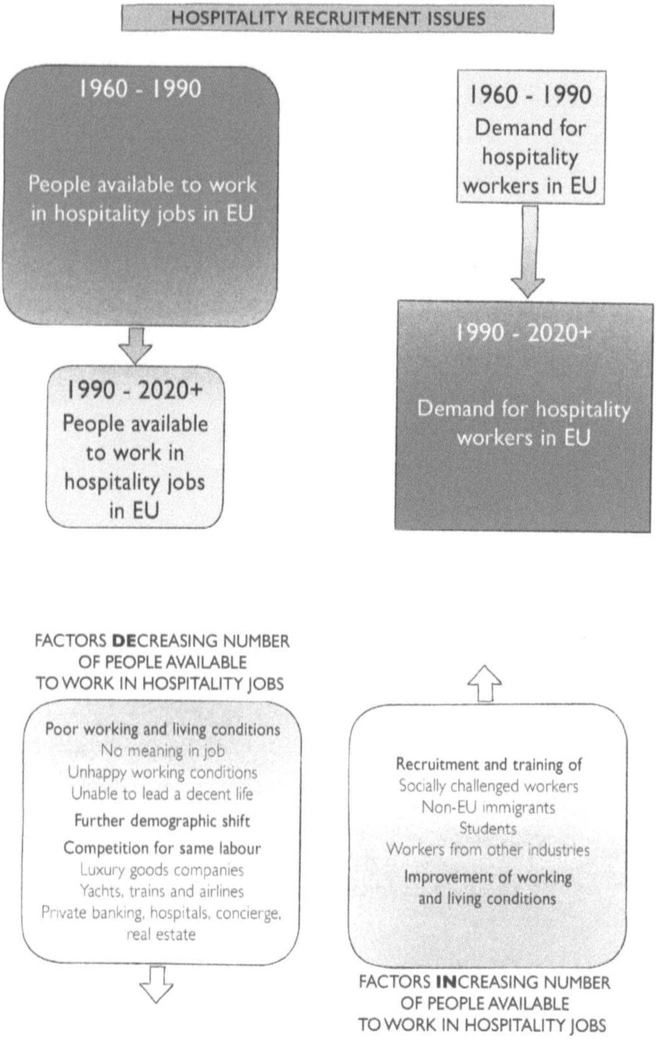

Demographics × Brexit × COVID

But the problem is not just limited to the UK. Across Europe, countries including Spain, Germany, Portugal and Greece, all face declining populations. Fertility rates (the average number of children born per woman) in these nations now hovers around 1.2, far below the 2.1 required to maintain a stable population. The EU average also sits stubbornly low, at 1.5.

Beyond Europe, Japan remains the global leader in population ageing, with a fertility rate of 1.26. Fifty years ago, Japan recorded two million births; by 2024, that number had dropped to 686,000. Farms and businesses close daily for lack of labour. So, what are Japan's options? One might be to supplement the workforce with labour from China, Korea, or Taiwan. But there, fertility rates are even lower: Korea (0.79 in 2022), Taiwan (0.87) and China (1.09). These countries are unlikely and in some cases, unwilling, to offset Japan's workforce decline.

C.A.E. Goodhart and Manoj Pradhan explore these realities in their thought-provoking book The Great Demographic Reversal. One conclusion is inescapable: over the next 30 years, advanced-ageing economies will face a significant shortage of local staff. The age pyramid data is unmistakable, clear and compelling in its implications.

As hoteliers, we should take the time to examine this data, country by country and consider the implications. It's both sobering and fascinating. In the EU, the working-age population has been shrinking for 20 years and will continue to do so for the next 20.

Immigration: Solutions and Fall-Out

If demographic decline is unavoidable, then the real question becomes how societies and industries like hospitality, choose to fill the gap. So far, the only viable solution to counteract fewer young people appears to be immigration. In ageing economies, the proportion of workers born elsewhere, Africa, Asia, South America, will inevitably increase. As we're witnessing in many countries, this shift is already provoking significant political tensions.

Singapore confronted this challenge earlier than most. In 2015, Prime Minister Lee Hsien Loong openly acknowledged the dilemma facing every government in the EU today:

> *"There are no easy choices on managing immigrants and foreign workers. There are trade-offs. If we have no foreign workers, our economy suffers, our own lives suffer. If we have a lot of foreign workers, the economy will do well, but we face other social pressures, other problems."*

Ultimately, the Singaporean government yielded to populist pressure and imposed restrictions on foreign worker arrivals. The result? For years, Singapore hotels reported 25% job vacancy rates. Since then they have adjusted their services, reduced restaurant operating hours and began investing in technological solutions like automation and robotics. Is this a glimpse into our future?

Of course, Singapore's tightly managed, one-party state model differs fundamentally from the political realities of European democracies, where immigration debates are more diffuse, contested and fragmented. Despite this, it may still foreshadow the kinds of structural strains Europe will face as shrinking youth populations make talent ever harder to find and train. But immigration alone cannot resolve all the pressures hospitality faces; for even when roles are filled, the question remains whether those jobs provide a standard of living that makes them worth keeping.

Part Three
The Living Standard Challenge

Living Standards are Slipping

When a hotel opens in India, Indonesia, or Thailand, dozens of people apply for each job. Those lucky enough to be selected will often earn significantly more than their peers. In these regions, hospitality jobs are considered highly attractive. The less favourable alternatives? For many, unemployment, farming, fishing, or factory sweatshops, despite the huge growth of economies in the Global South over recent years.

In the Global North, the picture can be quite different. One of the core issues is that real wages in hospitality and other service sectors, have not kept pace with the cost of living over the past forty years. This is largely due to the fact that productivity in the service sector has not increased at the same rate as in other industries; especially since the tech, finance and globalization booms. As a result, wages in service roles sit in the bottom quartile, making these jobs less and less appealing financially, particularly in an era in which the cost of living only continues to rise.

In 1975, a headwaiter at a luxury hotel in London could afford a mortgage on a house in North London. By 1995, a Food & Beverage Manager would barely have been able to afford a mortage on a similar home on the same street. Today, the General Manager would struggle to finance that same property without a substantial down payment. In 1975, the average house in the UK cost four times the average annual salary. But by 2022, that figure had more than doubled, with a house costing nine times the average salary.

HOUSE PRICES AS A MULTIPLE OF AVERAGE EARNINGS

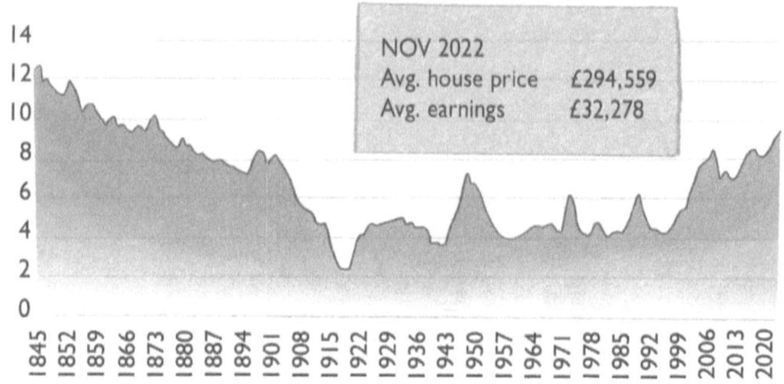

Source: Schroders, "What 175 years of data tell us about house price affordability in the UK", published in 2023

For service workers in major cities, increasingly dominated by highly paid professionals in high-productivity industries, maintaining a decent standard of living has become increasingly difficult. Building a long-term career in a sector known for low wages is harder than ever. Even for successful hotel employees in London, it can take a decade of steady progress, hard work and promotions before life becomes reasonably comfortable and even then, it often means choosing between a long commute or a cramped flat. Until then, shared housing is the norm. Under such precarious conditions, how can young workers even begin to think about starting a family?

Changing Priorities and Perks

In 1998, The Savoy Group, which included The Savoy, Claridge's, The Connaught and The Berkeley, was acquired by international investors, marking a shift in ownership and style of governance.

From 1941 to 1992, the group had been shaped by the values of Sir

Hugh Wontner, the hotelier and politician. Under his leadership, the Savoy had set the gold standard for five-star hotels in London, but the new owners had a different approach, shaped less by long-term stewardship and more by modern financial discipline.

Wontner had believed in providing for his staff and over the years, he acquired residential properties near the hotels. The Savoy had 28 staff rooms overlooking the Queen's Savoy Hill chapel, a staff house adjacent to The Lanesborough housed dozens and the top floor of Claridge's accommodated chambermaids and housekeepers. The front office manager at Claridge's stayed with the Savoy Group for over 20 years, partly thanks to the perks of staff housing in Holland Park.

When the new owners and their advisors took control, the housing was increasingly seen as underperforming real estate. From a modern financial perspective, this logic was sound: it made sense to liquidate these valuable assets.

It just so happened that around the same time, Chef Anton Edelmann began to struggle to recruit staff. The timing was coincidental, but the longer-term consequences have become clear: the perception that hospitality jobs are of low value and the reality that they no longer provide a viable standard of living is now a serious, structural problem for the industry.

This shift from long-term stewardship to short-term financial logic marked more than just a change in perks, it reflected a broader industry transformation, one that would soon reshape the very idea of the Grand Hotel.

Part Four
The Industry Structure Challenge

The Legacy of the Grand Hotel

A true Grand Hotel is a self-contained world. It offers a vast array of services to its guests. In the Grand Hotel, you can eat, sleep, drink, socialise, celebrate, exercise, relax and much more.

In the best Grand Hotels staff often stayed for decades. Guests returned generation after generation. Each Grand Hotel had its own art de vivre, its own unmistakable personality, whether it was The Savoy or Claridge's in London, Suvretta House in St. Moritz, or Plaza Athénée in Paris.

The Ritz in Paris, for example, was a vibrant hub for the literary and cultural life of the city. César Ritz designed it in 1909 to feel like a home for his loyal clientele who followed him from hotel to hotel. Marcel Proust once defined "Heaven" as "to be looked after like at the Ritz." Hemingway said that whenever he imagined the afterlife, it took place at the Ritz.

These Grand Hotels, mostly built between the late 19th and early 20th centuries, weathered two world wars, a major depression, post-war reconstruction and financial crises. Over time, many declined, unable to modernise or refurbish and became targets for acquisition by large hotel groups.

As the industry expanded and optimised for profitability, these iconic properties were swept into global portfolios, often losing what had made them magical places, as they were remade, centralised and rationalised alongside the rest of the portfolio's hotels.

Centralisation and Rationalisation

During this time, it made sense for the head office managers overseeing multiple hotels, including Grand Hotels, to rationalise the properties in their portfolios. The first step was to centralise key functions. This meant that operations including strategy, branding, finance, IT, training, marketing, sales, SOPs, revenue management and more were pulled out of individual hotels and moved to corporate HQs.

On some level this rationalisation worked. Standards improved, processes were aligned and the bottom line grew healthier, delighting CFOs. But then came the next wave. Head Offices identified more opportunities to improve profitability. As many capable third-party providers had entered the market, why not outsource? With outside experts running operations, in-house management could be leaner and more revenue-focused. Housekeeping, restaurants, bars, spas and security could all be handed over. And outsourcing, too, proved financially successful, but the cracks were starting to show.

With centralisation and outsourcing completed, the in-house hotel team was left managing the day-to-day rooms division. Although the hotel's complexity had been greatly reduced, Head Office spotted another opportunity. Managing a simplified unit just didn't require top-tier managerial talent any more. So why pay high salaries for roles that no longer demanded such expertise? Managerial costs were cut and once again, the CFOs were pleased.

By now, the Grand Hotel had now undergone three waves of rationalisation. It had been transformed into a lean, simplified operation that made sound financial sense at every turn. But what was left? The once-majestic Grand Hotel had become a Tiny Hotel. A shopping mall in disguise. Multiple independent businesses under one roof, each with its own goals, with few shared purposes. A tiny core team remained, responsible mostly for room operations.

Skills, intelligence and creativity had all migrated, to head offices, to consultants, to outsourced companies.

Self-Disruption

But how appealing is working in a Tiny Hotel?

Ask a group of students at a top hospitality school. Fewer than 10% say they want to work in hotels. Most would prefer to join corporate offices, consulting firms, specialists, or move into adjacent luxury sectors. In other words, they want to go where the real influence lies. Perhaps where constraints are fewer, too.

In an era when it's harder than ever to recruit and guest expectations have never been higher, we can question whether the decision to hollow out the Grand Hotel, draining it of its intelligence, substance and soul, ever truly made sense?

Some CFO's spreadsheets may still say yes. But Clayton Christensen, Harvard professor and author of The Innovator's Dilemma, might say otherwise. He'd call this a textbook case of self-disruption, a strategic narrowing that opens the door for new players to re-imagine the model altogether.

What's Lost in the Process?

To see the full cost of this self-disruption, we have to look beyond the balance sheets and ask what has quietly disappeared inside the hotel itself. Because for today's hotel staff, the holistic understanding of how a hotel works is slipping away. Entire departments are missing. Managers are absent. Career paths are increasingly precarious. It's like lifting the bonnet of a high-tech car: you stare at a sealed engine, no idea how the parts connect, or what to do when something breaks down.

Intelligence has left the building. The people who analyse and the people who deliver no longer sit in the same meeting rooms. In such a fragmented structure, where does ownership of the guest experience come from?

Would it not be thrilling, for young hospitality professionals and seasoned team members alike, to work side by side, solving real problems, improving the guest journey and reimagining what a Grand Hotel can be? Yes, this would be a return to the traditional but it would also be a more sustainable, future facing model, where the Grand Hotel can once again flourish and thrive, a place of magic once more.

Part Five
Training Challenge

The Reality of New Recruits

One of the most pressing challenges of the labour crisis is the changing profile of people considering work in hospitality. There are signs that future recruits may be less educated and less experienced and this skills gap has become even more pronounced since Covid.

So how do you structure your training when recruits need to learn so much, just to be able to meet ever increasing guest expectations? There are two sides to this coin: savoir-être (attitude) and savoir-faire (skills) and more recruits than ever are entering the industry without either. Many don't speak the local language. Through no fault of their own they may not understand, or be completely foreign to, local customs and culture. And on some days, this may be as good as it gets. The person in front of you may be the best available candidate: willing, kind, but not yet equipped for the demands of the job.

Surveys of hotel training strategies show that while training can evolve quickly, particularly with AI-driven tools, this is mainly true in large groups. Overall, skills training is relatively well-developed. But interpersonal judgement, social skills and the ability to form human connections are much harder to teach or train. AI-powered avatar videos can offer some preparation, but real emotional intelligence training requires real interactions.

And yet even as technical skills can be taught; we must never lose sight of what guests ultimately care about most. They want results, a smooth check-in, a great cup of coffee, a flawless restaurant booking. But they also want connection, a brief yet meaningful human interaction. And above all, they want "The Experience" a signature moment that awakens, surprises and delights. Something that breaks the routine, stays with them, that elevates the ordinary.

This is no small feat, especially in luxury hospitality.

Whatever mix of online, VR, or avatar-based learning we deploy, staff will still need in-person sessions to progress and cross key behavioural thresholds. That's where a real challenge lies. One that requires a mindset-shift.

When you want to train people, you need to pull them away from the front desk, the concierge, or the restaurant. Every hotel training manager will tell you the same story:

- "We organise training, but people don't show up."
- "We'd love to train more people, but departments won't release them".
- "Department heads wait for quiet periods to send staff to training, but since they're also responsible for payroll costs, they use that time to send people on holiday."

Why is that happening in every hotel? There's no budget provision in the payroll for training time. Somehow the head of department has to magically 'find' the time and gets caught in a Faustian dilemma. Do they sacrifice the training? (I don't have anyone available to go on a training session today'). Do they sacrifice quality of delivery? ('I am running the show without an adequate number of team members'). Do they sacrifice finances? ('I am expected to run lean year-round, managing costs with precision'). It's a challenging situation.

As a result, around the world, training sessions are getting shorter, more basic and increasingly delivered through automated tools, just like in every other service business.

Taking Stock and Training for the Future

So, what do we know? Demographics are not in our favour and the trend is set to worsen over the next 15 to 20 years. At the same time, international tourism is expected to grow by another 50%. Immigration could offer some relief by helping to fill the widening labour gap, but it can bring political challenges and practical difficulties due to cultural, social and educational differences. Recruiting, integrating and retaining this workforce will therefore require significant effort and political capital.

At the same time, the income gap between hospitality workers and knowledge workers is set to widen further, particularly in major European financial centres such as Paris, London and Milan. Hence, the ability to live a decent life in the sector may continue to be a challenge. Additionally, competition between industries and nations for a shrinking pool of talent will also intensify.

All this comes after a period in which large hospitality corporations have, perhaps unintentionally but certainly systemically, contributed to the de-skilling of many roles, streamlining operations at the cost of purpose and meaning. Now that much of this rationalization is behind us, perhaps the moment has come to rebalance towards a renewed sense of purpose, more attuned to a changing world.

The hospitality industry is facing a new reality, one where the traditional pipelines of talent, experience and cultural understanding can no longer be relied upon. The people stepping into guest-facing roles today are often untrained, unfamiliar with the setting and unaware of what excellence looks like. Many are doing their best, but they are entering a world of high expectations with almost no preparation. This isn't a temporary blip. It's the environment we now operate in. And it demands a new mindset.

We can no longer assume that staff arrive with the right skills, language, attitude, or cultural fluency. We must build these from the ground up, patiently, consistently and with intent. Not with generic online modules or surface-level workshops, but with real investment in live training, strong local leadership and a company culture that values development as much as delivery.

Have training departments adapted? Not yet, or not fully might be the honest answer at the time of writing. Until training is seen as an engine of the operation, we will continue to fall short and guests will continue to quietly lower their expectations. But with the right focus, the right priorities and the right support, there is real opportunity here.

We see countless ways to re-engage our teams, to attract new talent and to inspire long-term careers in what remains one of the most human and rewarding professions. We must remind ourselves and communicate clearly to others, that when done right, hospitality is not just a job. It is a craft, a calling and in many ways, one of the most gratifying careers there is. For at its core, it's about creating joy, building relationships and delivering moments of true connection. That's the essence of hospitality and it's a message that must be at the heart of our strategy.

Having set the stage, we can now turn to solutions. Now the question becomes: what can we actually do?

Part Six
From Scarcity Thinking to System Building

If the last section outlined the scale of the problem, this one asks us to think differently about solutions; should we keep fighting over a shrinking pool of talent, or change the system itself? This is a particularly interesting conundrum for hoteliers today: continue competing for the same limited pool of talent, an ever-shrinking resource with rising competition, or work to expand the pool, reducing reliance on human resources through better processes, IT and AI. This is not a theoretical question. It's the practical dilemma facing every business that wants to thrive in a talent-scarce, service-intensive environment.

Luxury vs Hospitality: Competing for Talent

One of the most immediate ways to rethink the system is not about technology at all, but about people, specifically, how we attract and compete for talent in the first place. Within this the first objective is simple in principle but hard in practice: stop the talent pool from shrinking further. That means making hospitality more desirable to the people who will soon matter most: young professionals choosing their career paths.

Revealing research here comes from Institut Montaigne, a respected French think tank. In its April 2025 survey on the work aspirations of 16-to-30 year-olds (students and early-career professionals), one sector emerged clearly as the most desirable: The Luxury Industry, ranking #1 out of 14 sectors.

Hospitality? It came in at #10, just below supermarkets. This raises a strategic question, is luxury hospitality part of the Luxury sector, or the Hospitality sector? Should it be ranked #1 or #10? How young talent perceives the answer to that question is bound to shape the future of the industry. However, the sector is ranked, luxury goods companies will be mining the same talent pool as luxury hotels.

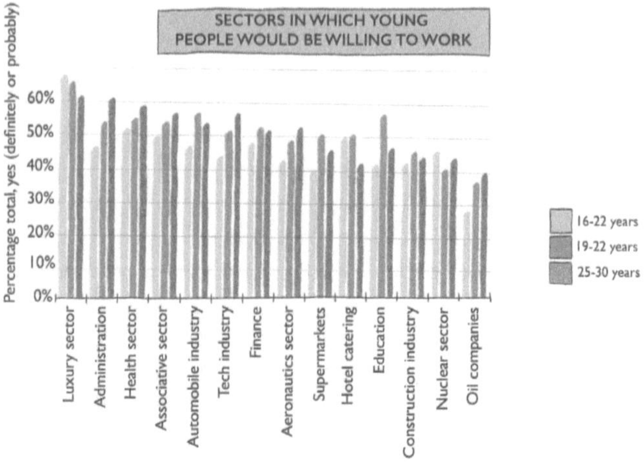

Source: AEF Info, "After the luxury sector, the civil service is the sector to which 16-30 year olds feel most attracted (Institut Montaigne)", published in 2025.

Competing with Luxury Goods Companies

Luxury hospitality is often compared to the luxury goods industry, but there is a fundamental difference between the two. In 1968, American psychologist Frederick Herzberg published one of the most widely read Harvard Business Review articles of all time: "One More Time, How Do You Motivate Employees?". In it, Herzberg introduces the two-factor theory of motivation. He distinguishes between intrinsic motivators (what truly motivates people) and extrinsic motivators (also called hygiene factors, or what prevents dissatisfaction). These two categories are not opposites on a single scale but operate independently. For example: wearing an ill-fitting or unattractive uniform can demotivate an employee. However, a perfectly tailored uniform will not actively motivate them, it simply avoids the negative effect. It doesn't inspire better performance; it just removes a point of dissatisfaction.

According to Herzberg, intrinsic motivators include achievement, the work itself, responsibility and personal growth. Hygiene factors, by contrast, include company policies, supervision, interpersonal relations, working conditions, salary and job security. For hospitality professionals, Herzberg's insight is particularly powerful because it reminds us that true motivation doesn't come from paychecks or perks alone, but from the craft of service, the pride of doing the work well, the responsibility of caring for others and the chance to create moments of real human connection, the very things that make hospitality meaningful. This distinction is crucial, because arguably it sets the stage for understanding why hotels and luxury goods companies compete for the same graduates, yet offer profoundly different kinds of motivation and meaning.

Luxury Hospitality vs. Luxury Retail

Between these sectors competition for top talent is intense and luxury retail companies increasingly compete directly with hotels for graduates. At elite hotel schools like Lausanne and Les Roches Crans-Montana, recruiters from luxury brands including LVMH, Richemont and Kering are regular visitors. Their presence is prominent, with logos on campus walls and strong recruitment programmes. Why? Because the package they offer is often more attractive: higher entry-level salaries, better working conditions, evenings and weekends off and predictable schedules. The appeal is obvious. Luxury is luxury, so why not choose the more comfortable path?

Here's the key difference. In a luxury goods company, the product, like a handbag, is the client's primary motivator. The staff and service are hygiene factors: expected, but not the reason for the purchase. In luxury hospitality, it's the opposite. The physical "product" (design, rooms, facilities) plays a supporting role. The team and the service they deliver are the intrinsic motivators. The people create the experience. They are the brand. This difference is profound when it comes to meaning.

This means that employees in luxury retail mainly maintain hygiene factors, supporting the sale of the product, but in luxury hospitality, employees are the experience. They sit at the top of the pyramid, not the base. Their work can create joy, connection and meaning. The satisfaction of making someone's day, of creating memorable moments, this is uniquely human and uniquely powerful.

As Antoine de Saint-Exupéry wrote in Terre des Hommes (Wind, Sand and Stars):

> *"There is only one true luxury in life, that is human relations."*

Not handbags.

Next Steps

Perhaps the key question is, how do we position luxury hospitality as one of the most exciting segments of the luxury world? How do we tell the story that this is where meaning and motivation live, not just polish and glamour?

The answer starts by recognizing and celebrating the human element, what makes hospitality truly luxurious and ensuring our teams feel it too.

Enlarging the Labour Pool in Ageing EU Economies

If luxury hospitality's strength lies in its people, their care, creativity and connection, then the next question is obvious: where will those people come from in an era of shrinking local labour pools and rising competition for talent? Not only that, but if hospitality workers are no longer entering from traditional pipelines in sufficient numbers, where will the next generation come from?

Possibilities include:

- Immigrants from Africa, the Middle East, South America and Asia
- Local universities, where students may seek limited hours of work

- Older adults, supplementing their income due to gaps in pensions or medical insurance
- Artists and creatives, picking up shifts to make ends meet as debt-laden governments reduce cultural funding and subsidies.
- People from all walks of life looking to find a new career path.

  The proportion of workers from these groups will only grow but for now let's begin with the most complex issue: immigration and integration.

Immigration vs Integration

In Europe, public and political discourse tends to revolve around immigration, often framed as a problem to manage. But what if the focus shifted? From immigration as an issue to integration as a solution.

Firstly, does integration work? The evidence suggests yes and powerfully so, when it's thoughtfully planned and handled with clear intent.

The German Example: Courage over Convenience

In 2015, Angela Merkel made a career-defining decision: she opened Germany's borders to nearly a million Syrian refugees. She staked her entire political legacy on doing what she felt was "the right thing to do." It wasn't easy. The challenge was immense, particularly the task of integrating a large population from a vastly different cultural background, most of whom didn't speak German. Acquiring language skills was therefore identified as priority number one for integration.

Policymakers also looked beyond short-term logistics to long-term macro needs. Germany's ageing population was facing a severe shortage of nurses and young people were not entering the profession in sufficient numbers. So the government created a programme to help train Syrian refugees as nurses. Today, over 10,000 former Syrian refugees work in German hospitals and care homes.

Germany chose the hard path.
It took political risks.
It invested.
It grew the labour pool.

And in the end, it worked, for the refugees, for the elderly they now care for and for the country.

The Swiss Example: Business as Usual

Now contrast that with Switzerland. Let's begin with the canton of Geneva. Roughly 70% of its nurses are foreign born, with most trained in neighbouring France. Why? Because Geneva no longer has the capacity (or candidates) to train enough nurses locally.

In Switzerland, nurses earn double what they would in France, just across the border. And yet, France itself faces its own nursing shortages. So, while France trains nurses, Switzerland attracts them away with higher salaries. The result? Switzerland benefits, without bearing any of the training or integration costs.

This same pattern exists in other Swiss regions, where Italian-speaking cantons recruit nurses from Italy and German-speaking regions attract German nurses.

It's a business-as-usual strategy. While Germany takes risks, absorbs political pressure and commits to integration, Switzerland simply buys talent trained elsewhere. Is that sustainable? Is it ethical?

As hoteliers, we face a similar decision: either continue competing for a shrinking pool of candidates, paying ever more for fewer qualified people, or step up, reframe the challenge and help enlarge the labour pool through training, support and integration. The first option may seem easier, but only the second offers long-term resilience, reputation and real contribution to our industry and society.

Part Seven
Redefining Work: Meaning, Mindset and Modern Hospitality

To help us navigate this decision let us take a detour to Japan, a country that sits furthest along the demographic curve with its shrinking population and dwindling labour market. Its experience is a window into the future for many ageing economies.

Historically, in contrast to the problems in modern hospitality that we've outlined, Japanese workers often stayed in their workplace for decades and much of their training happened organically, through observation, immersion and slow assimilation. It wasn't unusual to hear of 10-year training paths for sushi chefs. In fact, just learning to cook rice might take three years.

Take the Ryokan, a traditional Japanese inn. Some have existed for over 500 years. Many team members spent and some still spend, their entire career and even their entire life, within a single Ryokan. Getting to know the job in a traditional ryokan just takes years and succession has to be perfectly orchestrated over decades. At a Ryokan, meals are not served in dining rooms. Instead, elaborate multi-course dinners and breakfasts are served in the intimacy of the guest's room, accompanied by drinks and often paired with stories that help bring local traditions to life.

This entire experience is orchestrated by the Okami, the woman in charge of the guest's stay and often the Ryokan itself. She sets the table, serves the meal, clears the dishes and gently interacts with the guests. She must be able to read the mood perfectly, adapting her tone, presence and rhythm on each visit.

When the staffing pipeline breaks down, there is no short or easy answer. It can't be treated business as usual. Neither in terms of recruitment, there are no Okamis to be hired off the shelf, nor in the way the service is offered to the guests.

The question is, how long do we try to maintain the business-as-usual system and when is a mindset shift required? Sometimes, the latter is inevitable and this is what happened in a resort near Kyoto.

Hoshino Resort: A Mindset Shift

Faced with an acute, demographically driven challenge to traditional Japanese hospitality standards, a mindset shift became essential. One of the most striking solutions comes from Kyoto's Arashiyama district, at the Hoshino luxury resort. Here Mr. Hoshino built the resort around the staffing challenge. He rejected the constraints of Ryokan tradition and embraced a new paradigm.

He knew most recruits would lack experience and formal training. They'd want jobs that were fun, enriching and not overly repetitive. He also understood that younger people are less willing to endure physically taxing roles. It was time to look at the problem from some new angles, a shift of mindset that enabled a series of new solutions.

Shift 1:
Inspired by Hoshino, the resort's exceptional manager didn't force her staff into a rigid mould. Instead, she adapted her own framework to fit around their constraints, frustrations and needs.

Shift 2:
She redefined her role: no longer just oversight, but active staff support. Is room cleaning tough? "Yes and I'll do it with you." And she did, week after week, not for show but in solidarity. By sharing the work, she understood the problems firsthand, had the authority to fix them and earned her team's trust.

Shift 3:
She introduced multi-hat roles. Staff rotated between tasks, housekeeping in the morning, baristas by 11 a.m., servers in the afternoon, receptionists when needed. The variety made work more

stimulating, reduced monotony and built stronger teamwork and guest connections. Team members became multi-skilled hospitality artisans, discovering abilities that felt less like "just a job" and more like life skills they could carry with them forever.

Shift 4:

When guests arrived by boat, they were greeted by the sound of Rin Buddhist singing bowls, played by a "musician" in the garden. Guests paused, took photos and often struck up conversations. But the musician wasn't hired talent, earlier that day she might have been a chamber attendant, later a barista. Each day a new volunteer took the role, trained to play the bowls, enjoying the learning, the spotlight and the recognition. What began as a simple gesture became a daily ritual of creativity and pride.

When the situation has changed to the point where old solutions don't work any more, it is the entire 'system' that has to evolve. This may feel quite daunting, but examples like Hoshino show how good this can feel for team members and for guests.

Japan's situation may feel unique, but if we are looking for an example closer to home, then Amsterdam is a good place to continue our search.

How Good Is the Job? Zoku!

At Zoku, the brainchild of Hans Meyer, the creator of CitizenM, team dynamics have been reimagined with characteristic Dutch pragmatism. What sets Zoku apart is its radical rethinking of roles and relationships: blurring the lines between staff and guests, managers and team members, to create a culture of trust, ownership and genuine connection. These changes are captured in the story below.

When our colleague Janet checked into her room and discovered her kettle wasn't working, she logged the issue through the system. Jan from technical services arrived quickly. Unable to fix the kettle on the spot, he promised to return with a new one. Before leaving, he asked if he could help with anything else, even offering to bring her tea or coffee. That small gesture was a first for her.

The next morning at the rooftop breakfast, Janet saw Jan again, this time enjoying breakfast alongside guests, as staff and visitors share the same food and space. "Hey Janet, how's the kettle? Did everything work out? Did you sleep well?" he asked. Now that's a personal welcome. And does it really matter whether it comes from a maintenance engineer or a guest-relations manager?

Later, she met André, a young man serving coffee. A student from the Lausanne Hotel School andré explained that he had enjoyed his five-month internship at Zoku so much that he decided to stay on and delay returning to school by a year. Here was a young hotelier choosing day-to-day operations over one of the world's most prestigious hospitality programmes.

What did our young hotelier enjoy most? Being a responsible person from day one. The ability to participate and contribute fully. The lowering of barriers between managers and staff, staff and guests. The ability to please others every time he had an opportunity and the great open space he operated in. Light, sun-filled, full of plants and greenery. When jobs are that good, be it in Kyoto or Amsterdam, aspiring hoteliers won't leave the industry. Quite the opposite, they will become advocates.

That speaks volumes about the mindset shift at Zoku. Hans Meyer has truly adapted the work environment to suit the needs and realities of today's employees and it works.

Most importantly, it works for the guests. The atmosphere of conviviality and genuine hospitality is palpable, created by enthusiastic team members who clearly enjoy what they do and enjoy being around both their colleagues and their guests.

The stories of Hoshino and Zoku reveal a powerful truth: the future of hospitality depends not just on filling jobs, but on reimagining what those jobs can be. In an industry where people and service are the product, people are not just a resource, they are the experience. And when work is designed with meaning, flexibility and humanity at its core, the results can be extraordinary.

Rigid hierarchies and outdated expectations no longer serve today's workforce, or today's guests. Instead, what works is a series of mindset shifts: from control to collaboration, from tradition to adaptability and from standardization to personalization. Leaders who understand this are already building environments where staff can grow, contribute and truly thrive.

These aren't just feel-good stories; they are strategic imperatives. Because when the work is good, people stay. They advocate. They create magic for guests. And that, more than any design or amenity, is what sets great hospitality apart. So, if we want to attract the next generation of hoteliers, the question is no longer "How do we find the right people?" It's: "How do we become the kind of workplace great people are looking for?"

If reimagining the workplace is one side of the equation, reimagining education is the other, because without a strong pipeline of well-prepared people, even the best-designed jobs cannot thrive.

Part Eight
Education and a Cultural Shift

So, what happens when there is a market failure and a government failure? When traditional education systems and labour markets fail to supply qualified talent, the hospitality industry must step in, not only to recruit but to actively build the next generation of its workforce. That means training people from the ground up, shortening pathways into work and designing programmes and schools that match the urgency of industry needs, while also opening doors for those who have been excluded. Across Europe and beyond, we are seeing pioneering models that prove this is possible: from Michelin-starred chefs who open fast-track culinary schools for the unemployed, to social enterprises that blend hotels with training centres, to new academies designed not for entry-level staff but for managers themselves. These initiatives show that when business, local government and educators work together, the talent pool doesn't just grow, it is transformed.

Cuisine Mode d'Emploi

Thierry Marx is renowned in France and Japan as a Michelin-starred chef. Frequently seen on TV and heard on radio programmes, he is also a passionate advocate for good food and a committed activist. He thrives on tough challenges. Facing a shortage of qualified cooks, Marx chose not just to complain but to act. In 2012, in collaboration with local governments, regional and city councils, he launched a new kind of culinary school: Cuisine Mode d'Emploi.

In France, a traditional kitchen apprenticeship typically lasts around three years, far too long for an industry urgently in need of staff. It's also impractical for individuals who may be lacking training, need work immediately and find the idea of a three-year commitment daunting. Additionally, traditional culinary curricula were outdated and reforming them at a national level would take time. Moreover, the system failed to accommodate the realities of the people they hoped to reach.

So, Marx brought together a team of top chefs and asked a practical question: what must a new kitchen recruit know to get started, contribute meaningfully and earn a living?

The team decided to limit training to a maximum of three months. In that time, students would learn 80 essential techniques and 90 foundational recipes, including a three-week placement in a professional kitchen. The target group? Socially challenged individuals who could not find their own way in our society, both young and not so young. The outcome was remarkable, 88% of graduates found employment after the programme and left with a state-recognised certificate. The programme has been such a success that over the past decade, 12 new schools have opened.

The Good Group, Amsterdam

Another example of a successful training model is the Good Hotel, a pioneering social enterprise that blends high-end hospitality with a mission to empower individuals experiencing long-term unemployment. Founded in 2015 by Dutch entrepreneur Marten Dresen, the hotel initially operated on a floating platform moored in Amsterdam but later relocated to London.

At the heart of the hotel's mission lies the Good Training programme, an initiative designed to equip unemployed locals with the skills and experience needed to thrive in the hospitality industry. In partnership with local authorities, the hotel identifies individuals who have been out of work long-term and offers them a fresh start, regardless of their background, delivering inclusive recruitment.

Over the course of three months participants receive intensive training, with a focus on hands-on instruction across various aspects of hospitality, preparing them for employment both at the hotel and within the wider industry. Graduates are then offered employment opportunities including a three-month contract at the Good Hotel, with ongoing support to secure permanent roles with partner establishments, creating clear pathways to sustainable careers. In its first year, the programme trained over 100 participants, more than 70 of whom went on to secure permanent employment in hospitality.

The Good Hotel also operates as a non-profit, reinvesting all profits into its training programmes and partner NGOs. Its business model emphasizes measurable social outcomes over traditional financial returns, aiming to foster meaningful, lasting change in the communities it serves.

After its success in Amsterdam, the floating hotel moved to London, continuing its social mission. The Good Group has since expanded, including opening boutique hotels in Antigua and Guatemala, where it partners with local NGOs to provide education and vocational training. Through this innovative approach, the Good

Hotel demonstrates how businesses can embed social responsibility into their core operations, delivering tangible value to individuals and communities.

Much like *Cuisine Mode d'Emploi*, the Good Hotel's impact depended on the active engagement of many stakeholders, including city councils, educational boards, local hoteliers and academic partners such as The Hague Hotel School. In both cases, collaboration across sectors proved essential to achieving lasting results. But while these examples focused on training line staff, the need for education now extends further up the ladder, as managers, too, require new forms of development. That is precisely the gap KIHA (Kepler International Hospitality Academy) set out to address when it launched in September 2024.

The KIHA Academy Concept

Hoteliers, like their employees, are navigating a rapidly changing landscape of uncertainty, shaped by the forces we've discussed throughout this chapter. Yet most hotel managers are trained in hotel schools where curricula, case studies and courses are based on past research and experiences. Like most academic institutions, hotel schools are inherently slow to evolve. Updating and certifying academic programmes takes years, even in the best-case scenario. Unfortunately, this timeline no longer aligns with the pace and demands of today's tourism industry.

By the time hoteliers reach managerial positions, they have long left school behind and spent years, often decades, immersed in the business. But at this stage, they need time to pause, reflect, re-assess and reframe. However, business demands, financial pressures and personal or family responsibilities leave little room for reflection. In response to this challenge the authors decided it was time to act, launching an academy dedicated to training and more often, retraining, leaders. The goal, to help reshape hoteliers' mindsets and guide them toward regenerative models that serve all stakeholders.

In the academy, participants are guided through a reflective process and emerge with a renewed vision, prepared to lead their teams and companies in the right direction while acting in the best interests of all stakeholders. Unsurprisingly, managers who attend the KIHA course often realise they must change course themselves, as they begin to question long-held goals, ambitions and practices.

Working on one's mindset is no easy task. It demands courage and persistence. As a teacher or coach, one can only accompany people on their journey, nudging here, suggesting there, but the true effort comes from the managers themselves.

This challenge is not limited to individual leaders. It reflects a broader gap in the systems that are meant to prepare and support them. When education and labour structures fall behind, the responsibility inevitably shifts to businesses themselves to create the conditions for learning and renewal. In such moments, businesses and other stakeholders can no longer wait for "someone else" to step in.

We must come together as responsible citizens and lead the way. Opening schools and developing integrated training programmes are powerful steps toward addressing these gaps, shaping the future and reimagining training within the sector.

Part Nine
Reimagining Training as a Strategic Investment

In previous sections, we've explored the urgent need to protect and expand the hospitality talent pool, by positioning hospitality as a desirable, meaningful career and by opening the doors to non-traditional workforce segments. But doing either of those effectively requires a fundamental rethink of how we develop people. At the heart of this process of rethinking lies a neglected but vital question:

What if the way we train our existing staff, rather than who we hire, becomes one of our greatest competitive advantages?

More radically, what if training were not a cost to manage, but a profit centre to grow? This idea may sound far-fetched at first, but in reality, it may be the most pragmatic and necessary mindset shift the hospitality sector can make.

Training Today: Under-resourced, Under-strategised and Under-valued

Let's start by looking honestly at how training is typically handled today. When a new team member arrives they are usually needed on the floor immediately. There may be some onboarding, a few shadow shifts and perhaps a checklist to complete, but structured learning is rare. The pressure of operations makes it nearly impossible to set aside real time for learning, reflection, or behavioural growth. Training is reactive. At best, it's focused on procedures. At worst, it's reduced to a form of "learning by osmosis" in a high-pressure environment.

But why is this the case? A major reason is both simple and systemic: we don't properly account for the real cost of training. Although most hotels maintain a training budget, which typically covers external courses, consultants, digital platforms, or printed materials, the largest and most expensive component, the time of the people being trained, is completely invisible in the budget. And because it's not tracked, it's not managed. It's as if it costs nothing.

This has serious consequences. Training sessions may be planned, but when the time comes, team members are unavailable. Every department is stretched. Operational pressures take precedence. And since no one ever sees the immediate financial impact of pulling someone out for two hours, it's easy to cancel or postpone the session entirely.

In short, training fails not because it isn't valued in theory, but because it isn't resourced in practice and because the value it provides is usually not immediately quantifiable.

Learning From Other Sectors: A Benchmark for Structured Development

Outside hospitality, more structured models for training are not only common, they're considered essential. Take the healthcare sector in Germany. As discussed previously, when the country welcomed nearly one million Syrian refugees in 2015, it faced a dual challenge: the integration of this refugee community and an ageing population with an acute shortage of nurses.

Germany's response was bold but strategic, introducing programmes where Syrian immigrants could enroll in state-supported nursing programmes where they worked four days per week and studied one day. That's 20% of their time devoted to structured learning, with clear pathways toward long-term contribution to the state and society and their own financial security. The process was not easy, as Syrian nurses had to navigate demanding coursework, new medical standards and the strain of adapting to a different culture and language. Yet, despite these challenges, the scheme has been widely regarded as a success; indeed without it, Germany's nursing infrastructure might well have buckled under the strain.

France's apprenticeship system offers another model. Apprentices typically spend one-third of their time at school and two-thirds at work. In higher education, master's students often alternate between three days of work and two days in school, equating to roughly 40% of their week in formal education.

Across all these models, structured, recurring, intentional learning time is seen as essential, not a luxury. What if hospitality adopted a similar standard?

A New Benchmark

Let's be conservative, let's take the lowest common denominator and then cut it in half, mindful of how tight margins are in our sector, leaving us with just half a day per week dedicated to training and development. That's 10% of a team member's time. In operational terms, it means employees are available 90% of the time but paid for 100% of their time, placing pressure on training to be truly effective and worthwhile. But the focus shouldn't be on whether we can afford to do this, but rather on whether we can afford not to. Because what's at stake is not just skill acquisition, it's staff engagement and retention, guest satisfaction, brand loyalty and operational excellence. If people are the heart of our business, their growth must be central to our strategy.

To consider what this would look like in practice, imagine a hotel with 250 staff, of which around 100 are in guest-facing roles such as front desk, restaurant service, housekeeping and concierge. With a one-day-per-week training commitment, roughly 10 front-line staff would be in training at any given time. This would require full-time trainers to deliver daily sessions across different departments and topics, supported by a coordinator to manage scheduling, training calendars, content alignment and logistics. It would also mean having dedicated training spaces designed for interaction, small-group work and immersive simulations, with sessions delivered in flexible formats, such as one- or two-hour modules, to minimise disruption and maintain operational flexibility.

This may sound resource-heavy. But consider what we expect from our teams: deep empathy, personal presence, multilingual communication and spontaneous problem-solving, sometimes all in a single guest interaction. These capabilities are not "extras." They are core competencies and they must be intentionally cultivated.

The Nature of Hospitality Training: Beyond Technical Skills

Much of the most impactful training in hospitality is not about tasks. It's about behaviour. How to truly listen to a guest. How to read a room. How to recover quality service after a misstep. How to exude calm, warmth and attentiveness under pressure. These are subtle, human skills and they're difficult to teach. Online platforms, AI avatars and simulation tools can support the basics, but real behavioural growth requires something else: time, reflection, challenge and support.

Ideally, this kind of training happens in small groups, no more than 8 to10 people, where every participant can be challenged individually and learn in community. It's closer to coaching than instruction. And it's essential if we want team members not just to execute, but to evolve.

So why don't we do it more in hotels?

There are two answers.

First, training is still viewed as a cost centre, an operational burden rather than a strategic lever. We remain tied to outdated assumptions and default to traditional financial metrics when making decisions. Second, many of us lack a vision for what high-impact training could look like. Perhaps we've never seen a model where training significantly enhances retention, improves guest satisfaction and ultimately feeds directly into profit margins.

But that model exists. In fact, it's already emerging, in forward-thinking hotels that treat people development as central to their value proposition.

If Design Deserves Investment, So Does Development

We, or our hotel's owners, often don't hesitate to spend on design, technology, or amenities, because we see a direct link to guest satisfaction and we can easily compare our product to competitors. But too often, we treat the people delivering those experiences as temporary assets rather than long-term investments.

But if we want to create consistently exceptional experiences, human, memorable, emotionally rich, we must invest in the humans who deliver them. That means putting training at the centre of the business model. And when we do that, not only does the quality of service improve, so does the quality of work.

And isn't that the essence of hospitality? To serve, to grow and to elevate. And that starts with our people.

Part Ten
Leading Decent Lives

If training is about nurturing professional growth, then ensuring our staff live decent lives is about nurturing the whole person and the two are inseparable in any vision of sustainable hospitality. After all, how can we expect staff to deliver exceptional service if their own basic needs for dignity, stability and belonging are not met?

In the hospitality industry, we talk a great deal about creating experiences, luxurious stays, seamless service and memorable moments. But too often, we overlook the people who make those experiences possible. What kind of lives do our workers lead? Can they afford to live where they work? Do they eat well, feel safe and belong to a supportive community?

These are not marginal questions. In fact, they go to the very heart of what hospitality really means. Leading a decent life, having access to stable housing, nourishing food, meaningful relationships and a sense of dignity, should not be a privilege reserved for guests alone. It should be the baseline expectation for our teams.

Just as we strive to make guests feel seen, valued and connected, we must show staff that our relationship with them matters too. Yes, it may be a professional, conditional relationship, but it must be one in which their fundamental needs are actively considered and cared for. For when employees feel this, they're more likely to bring the same warmth, attentiveness and commitment to the guests they serve. And yet, for many in our industry, these fundamentals are out of reach.

This section explores what it means to support "decent living" for hospitality workers, not as an abstract ideal, but as a practical, necessary and inspiring objective. Throughout we'll ask, what would it look like if we, as hoteliers, applied our creativity and resources not just to our guests' comfort, but to our employees' lives?

From factory towns in 18th-century France to food co-operatives in Brooklyn, from co-living spaces in Denmark to eco-neighbourhoods in Germany, we'll see that better living isn't only possible, it's been done before. And it can be done again.

To move forward on this path, let's take a moment to step away from hospitality and examine a compelling story that can reveal crucial insights.

Baccarat: Beyond the Furnace

This story is the story of the Baccarat workers, a community deeply entwined with the history of the Cristallerie de Baccarat, one of the most prestigious crystal manufacturers in the world. This story is not just about glass and craftsmanship, but also about how a rural French village became a thriving, tightly knit industrial and social community.

The Baccarat crystal factory was established in 1764 in the small town of Baccarat, in the Lorraine region of eastern France, under the authorization of King Louis XV. It was founded to stimulate the local economy and make use of the area's abundant natural resources, wood for fuel, silica for glassmaking and water for power, at a time in which France was seeking to expand its industrial might. As the factory grew, it drew workers and artisans from surrounding areas, forming the core of what would become a company-centred community.

The main workshop, the hot, glowing heart of the factory, became the centre around which the town organised itself. Homes were built for Baccarat's workers close to the factory, including modest but functional houses for glassblowers, cutters and other artisans, as well as more refined residences for engineers and managers. Many families remained at Baccarat for generations, passing down their skills and roles from parent to child, which fostered a strong sense of identity, pride and belonging. Alongside housing, the company and the town also developed a wide-ranging social infrastructure, including schools (with technical training options), churches, sports clubs, music groups, co-operative stores and communal kitchens, creating not just a workplace, but a thriving, close-knit community. It became more than a factory town, it was a living example of an industrial model, where the company played a role not only as employer but also as provider and cultural patron. A model that although paternalistic, was hugely impactful.

Although most Baccarat workers and their families led modest lives, they certainly lived decent lives and developed a sense of community and place and a security that lasted generations. Although Baccarat was founded more than 250 years ago there remains plenty we can learn from its story. It reminds us that when employers invest not only in jobs but in housing, culture and community, they can create ecosystems where people don't just work, they belong, thrive and build lasting futures.

The Park Slope Food Coop

After housing, access to healthy, nourishing food is often the next most important priority. An inspiring example comes from Brooklyn, New York, where a pioneering food initiative offers valuable lessons for how we might support hospitality workers in leading decent, dignified lives.

The Park Slope Food Coop (PSFC), established in 1973 in Brooklyn, New York, is one of the oldest and most prominent food co-operatives in the United States. It operates on a participatory model where members contribute labour to maintain the store's operations. At the heart of PSFC's model is the requirement that each adult member works a 2-hour and 45-minute shift every four weeks. These shifts cover a range of tasks, from stocking shelves and cashiering, to cleaning and administrative duties. It's a collective labour model that significantly reduces operational costs, allowing the Coop to offer products at lower prices than conventional supermarkets. This means that members typically benefit from reduced mark-ups, at just 21% over wholesale prices, compared to the typical 25–100% in traditional retail. For most that's a pretty good trade-off for the work they have to put in.

The Coop also places a strong emphasis on organic, local and environmentally friendly products, ensuring that its members have access to high-quality goods. If all this wasn't enough, the work that members do together fosters a strong sense of community, encouraging collaboration and shared responsibility. There are also plenty of educational opportunities on offer, central to the Coop's community-focused model, with regular workshops, events and resources promoting sustainable living and informed consumer choices. The Coop also aims to be financially accessible, offering reduced membership fees and investment requirements for individuals receiving income-based assistance. Overall, the Park Slope Food Coop's model not only provides economic benefits to its members but also cultivates a community-oriented environment centred on shared labour and mutual support.

With up to 17,000 members, the co-operative has more disposable man-hours than any other service business. Instead of being on a constant labour cost-cutting exercise as many businesses would be, the Coop team has a diametrically opposed approach, focused instead on what further services they could offer to enhance their members' lives.

The result? Park Slope Coop members love their shopping, their sense of agency and the burgeoning community they're part of. Who wouldn't? Coop members working that evening might help shoppers carry their bags home. They might offer to look after younger children while the parents do their shopping, or they might organise home delivery. Coop members working that evening are all part of the same community; teachers, lawyers, social workers, each personally invested in the project. No one is a stranger.

Fundamentally what PSFC shows is that when labour is a resource for good rather than a cost that must be slashed, life improves drastically. If food and belonging can be reimagined this way, so too can housing, which for many workers is the first and most urgent barrier to living with dignity.

Extending Hospitality to the People Who Deliver It

For anyone arriving in London, Paris, or virtually any major European city in search of housing, the process can be disheartening. Even after identifying a place you can afford, the obstacles often keep coming. Real estate agents may question your creditworthiness or reliability, demanding multiple guarantees. And what's waiting at the end of this exhausting journey? Usually, a small, probably underwhelming apartment in a distant neighbourhood. Worst of all, you'll be alone, physically and emotionally, at a time when support matters most.

Now, contrast this big city eco-system with how some communities approach the idea of housing and social integration. In Denmark, extensive research and innovation have gone into creating better models of community living. One of the clearest takeaways: your happiness is profoundly shaped by the community you live in. Isolation is among our greatest stressors; whereas connection, conversely, is a key ingredient of a fulfilling life. But it turns out that well-designed buildings alone, a nice lounge, a co-working space, a playground, aren't enough to create meaningful connections. What really makes the difference are the people whose role is to actively foster those connections: community managers.

This principle is also alive and well in Germany, particularly in Freiburg-im-Breisgau (as mentioned in chapter one). The city is known for its forward-thinking community initiatives, including the eco-neighbourhoods of Vauban and Rieselfeld. Both were developed with input from future residents and stakeholders, resulting in spaces where cooperation and mutual support are part of everyday life.

These communities don't just function, they flourish. Residents know each other, support one another and take part in regular events organised by the community itself, with the guidance of a community manager. It's a model of urban life where connection isn't left to chance, it's built in.

Dear hotelier, don't look away. At this point, you may be tempted to say: "That's lovely, but it doesn't apply to us, it's outside the scope of our business." Or perhaps: "We shouldn't interfere with employees' private lives." But here's the truth: many hospitality workers today cannot live decent lives. When it comes to the housing market, there's both a market-failure and a government-failure at play. And when that happens, someone else has to step in. Yes, this is a social project. And no, there's no viable alternative.

But what is a social project? By that we mean a process of deliberately shaping the conditions for people to live decently. In hospitality, it is the commitment to design housing, food systems and community life with the same imagination and care we devote to guest experiences, extending the promise of hospitality to those who deliver it.

Staff Accommodation: A Necessity not a Perk

So what can we do? Let's begin with the basics: safe, accessible and affordable staff accommodation. When done well, this offers four clear benefits:

1. A ready place to live from day one, meaning no frantic housing search.
2. A relief from overwhelming admin and financial stress.
3. An assurance of well-maintained, pleasant living conditions.
4. Reasonable, stable rent that fits within a modest income.

In fact, forward-thinking institutions are already showing the way. Take Imperial College London, for instance. Expanding on its experience with student housing, the university now offers staff accommodation as well. The properties are fully furnished and offered at up to 40% below market rates, prioritising proximity to campuses and transit. The goal? To ease the financial burden, strengthen staff retention and make urban living more viable for those contributing to the institution.

Likewise in Paris, the Four Seasons Hotel George V has partnered with co-living company La Casa to offer shared housing for employees. This arrangement eliminates much of the logistical burden and ensures a smoother transition for new hires. It's a strong response to the first three staff accommodation needs. But when it comes to affordability, the market still calls the shots. This raises a critical question: is outsourcing really the most visionary option? What if we aimed higher?

Hoteliers are experts at designing exceptional guest experiences. Why not apply that same creativity and attention to detail to staff accommodation and move beyond housing, toward community?

Drawing inspiration from Freiburg, Copenhagen and other community-driven living models, hospitality businesses can create co-living environments for their team members that offer far more than a bed and a roof.

These ideas shouldn't be all that strange, in many industries, companies already offer perks like travel cards, discounts, or gym memberships. The idea of staff accommodation as a key social project of the hotelier simply takes this a little further, addressing two of the biggest challenges for employees: finding housing and settling into a new city for work. In fact, big tech firms have embraced a similar model for years to attract and keep top talent; in hospitality we believe it could be an equally powerful tool for building loyalty, stability and shared purpose.

Building Belonging: The Deeper Value of Community

For young professionals in hospitality, community living provides not just comfort but essential emotional and social support.

The industry's irregular hours and high-pressure pace become more manageable when surrounded by peers who understand. In fact, community living reduces loneliness and fosters informal networking, peer mentoring, shared routines and life-long friendships.

For many workers, this isn't just a lifestyle preference, it's a lifeline. So, what do young people say they want to do during their downtime to recharge? They want to connect, enjoy entertainment and stay active. That's why well-designed co-living spaces should include a small gym, a cinema or game room and communal dining areas.

Alongside all this, and just as importantly, they should offer opportunities for both connection and privacy, "we time" and "me time."

Here again, the role of the community manager is key. To be optimised, communities need to be managed. This person helps facilitate introductions, nurture bonds and organise group activities. In a hospitality context, the Human Resources department could drive this initiative, identifying, training and incentivising team members to take on the role. After all, who better to care for the carers than those who already dedicate themselves to welcoming and serving your guests?

Also: would a luxury hotel really want to outsource something so central to its internal culture?

Food: The Original Social Project

Now let's talk about something just as fundamental, food. Up to half of hotel employees work in Food & Beverage. And in Europe especially, mealtime is community time. It's when bonds are built, stories are shared and cultures meet. Imagine a co-living space where team members cook together, share favourite dishes, organise communal meals and rotate chores and responsibilities.

With the support of a community manager, this can become an enriching, even joyful, experience. A shared kitchen with large ovens,

BBQs, communal tables and open layouts can support this kind of interaction. Even better? Create rituals, like design-your-own-pizza night, that staff look forward to. Rituals build culture and culture builds community.

Let's not forget the economics: food is expensive, good food even more so. Hotels can help their team members access 'better' food, food that's healthy, fresh and affordable, using their buying power with suppliers to enable staff to order cheaper food each week, much like the Coop. To ensure this is not just another burden on HR or management, staff members themselves could help coordinate food ordering and distribution, again taking inspiration from the Park Slope Food Coop model, where members share responsibilities to access affordable, high-quality food. By leveraging the hotel's purchasing power and engaging staff in shared, rotating roles, a sense of empowerment and ownership can grow, without adding pressure to daily operations.

The result? Better nutrition, stronger relationships and a deeper sense of belonging.

The Co-living Lab

Let's go one step further, from housing and food to the social. All those experiences that make life worth living. Through this social project we can reimagine how hospitality staff live, not just where they sleep, but how they move, connect and thrive. This can include bike and car-sharing programmes, local event passes, community outings, all things that add texture and joy to daily life. Remember, we're not just building homes. We're building a platform to help people live and thrive together.

A key part of this platform is what we might call the hotel's co-living 'lab', perhaps the most powerful educational and developmental tool at our disposal.

By creating co-living spaces for employees, hotels can offer more than a roof over their heads. These communities can become "co-living labs", living environments where ideas about well-being, sustainability and social connection can be actively tested and refined. Shared meals, peer mentoring, group rituals and bike-sharing programmes aren't just perks; they're experiments in building a better way to live and work.

Just as importantly, these spaces foster a sense of ownership and empowerment. Staff aren't passive tenants, they're invited to take part in the systems that make community life flourish, from coordinating food co-operatives, to managing shared mobility schemes, organizing events, or even stepping into the role of community manager. These contributions cultivate leadership, autonomy and a stronger sense of purpose at all levels.

The results can be powerful. Staff arrive more grounded, less stressed and emotionally supported. Team cohesion improves. Cultural awareness deepens. Turnover drops. And guests benefit in ways they can feel but may never see, through attentive service, warm interactions and a sense that care runs deep, both in front-of-house and behind the scenes.

When staff housing becomes a co-living lab, it does more than solve a little part of the housing crisis. It creates a new kind of hospitality ecosystem, one where those who serve are also nourished, connected and inspired, and where young people gain the confidence to take the initiative because they've learned, firsthand, what brings others joy. Of course, not everyone wants to live with their colleagues, but for those who do, especially younger team members starting out, the option can be invaluable. Even helping staff secure affordable housing nearby can make a huge difference, offering stability, shortening commutes and giving people the choice to be part of a supportive community without it being compulsory.

Ultimately these social projects, housing, food, mobility and community support, need not just be seen as a social investment. They're actually also a smart business strategy, allowing hoteliers to strengthen their teams while contributing to the wider well-being of the places they operate in. This isn't charity, it's a way of aligning commercial success with the creation of healthier, more resilient local communities, where staff feel rooted, valued and able to give their best.

Part Eleven
What about Staffing Costs?

Scenario:	**Future Staffing Strategy for Luxury Hotels**
Setting:	The boardroom, over cups of coffee.
Characters:	
General Manager:	Ambitious and forward thinking
Board Members:	Cautious by nature
The Chair:	Extra cautious by position

GM:	Thank you all for joining. Let's begin with our first agenda point; staffing. As we look ahead, it's clear that staffing costs will continue to rise, not just in terms of salaries, but also in the investment needed to recruit, train and groom talent to meet luxury service expectations. What's clear to me at least, is that the question isn't whether we'll spend more, but whether we can spend wisely.
Board Member 1:	Agreed and we can add to that the rising cost of developing staff with the right etiquette, language skills and emotional intelligence.
GM:	Precisely. But we also have an opportunity. From what I can tell AI and automation will

	absolutely help, particularly in non-guest-facing roles like housekeeping logistics, inventory, scheduling, even elements of F&B prep. I think it's in these places where we can really gain cost efficiencies.
Board Member 2:	But that still leaves front-line workers.
GM:	Yes and that's where we should double down in my opinion. I think we can all agree that in luxury hospitality, our service team is the brand. The warmth of welcome, the emotional attentiveness, the anticipation of needs, those are not easily replicated or automated.
Board Chair:	So, if I understand you correctly, you're suggesting we lean into technology to save on the back-end and reinvest those savings into high-quality, high-touch staff development at the front?
GM:	Exactly. I think the future of luxury will be all about financing the delivery of exceptional, personalised service. What I mean by that is that every team member who interacts with a guest becomes a point of differentiation. I know we probably can't out-tech the mass-market chains, but we can out-human them. And I truly believe that's where loyalty and premium pricing will be won.

Conclusion: Mindset Shifts

If this and the previous chapter have made one thing clear, it's that we can no longer meet tomorrow's challenges with yesterday's thinking. The systems, assumptions and habits that sustained us for decades are no longer fit for purpose. To move forward, we must shift our mindset. Not incrementally, but fundamentally.

Here are the shifts we believe we must make as hoteliers:

1. From competing for talent → to growing the talent pool

For too long, we've all been fishing in the same small pond, looking for candidates who tick every box from day one. But that pool is shrinking fast. We must broaden who we consider and invest in helping people grow into the roles we need. Growing the pool is no longer optional, it's essential.

2. From staff as a cost → to people as the product

In luxury hospitality, our team is not behind the brand, they are the brand. Our guests don't come for the fixtures or the technology. They come for the warmth, the welcome, the attention to detail. We need to stop treating people as a line item and start seeing them as the experience we're selling.

3. From ad-hoc training → to structured, strategic development

We say training matters, but we rarely give it the time, space, or budget it deserves, especially the hidden cost: the labour hours of the people being trained. If we want consistent, emotionally intelligent service, we need proper behavioural training, delivered in small groups, with proper follow-up. Not once a year, but every week.

4. From rigid roles → to empowered, multi-skilled teams

Today's talent wants variety, purpose and a powerful sense of agency. Let's design jobs that rotate. Let's give people the space to learn new skills and shine in new ways. When one person is a housekeeper in the morning and a barista in the afternoon, they don't just avoid burnout and boredom, they build pride, versatility and deeper guest relationships.

5. From waiting for schools → to becoming the school

If the pipeline is broken, we have to fix it ourselves. That means opening our own academies, partnering with communities, building fast-track training models and creating real alternatives to traditional hospitality education. We can't afford to sit back and hope the system catches up. We must become part of a better system.

6. From filling jobs → to redesigning work

The best jobs today are not just well-paid, they're well-designed. Flexible, meaningful and connected to something bigger. If we want people to stay, we need to offer more than shifts and salaries. We need to offer a sense of belonging, the chance to grow and work that feels meaningful.

7. From fragmented operations → to rebuilt identity

Many of us have outsourced and centralised our way into operational efficiency, but we've lost something along the way; culture, coherence and internal pride. It's time to reintegrate, to bring departments back into the fold and to create strong, cohesive teams that know and trust each other.

8. From delegated culture → to shared leadership

Culture doesn't live in an HR manual. It lives in the way we speak, lead, train and support every day. It's the General Manager rolling up their sleeves. It's the head of housekeeping mentoring a new hire. It's the sous-chef taking time to teach a new trainee how to plate with care. We can't delegate culture. We all carry it. We all shape it. And we all have a role to play.

9. From jobs as transactions → to hospitality as a social project

We're not just employers, we're community builders and that means our hotels can offer more than a paycheck. They can offer meaning, mentorship, housing, food, stability and dignity. When we treat hospitality as a social project, we don't just attract talent, we change lives. Because people who live decently, stay. People who feel seen and supported, perform better. When we invest in people beyond their job description, when we help them live well, we elevate the entire experience, for everyone.

10. From staff accommodation → to co-living labs for growth and belonging

Too often, we see housing as a problem to solve, or worse, a box to tick. But what if it were a lever for transformation? Let's move beyond basic staff housing toward co-living environments that support growth, well-being and community. Places where team members don't just sleep, but connect, learn and live decently. Where development happens informally, trust builds naturally and isolation is replaced with shared purpose. A co-living lab is more than accommodation. It's a signal of care. A training ground for life. And it's a strategic investment in the people shaping our guest experience.

This is the shift. It starts with us.

These 10 shifts aren't theoretical. They're already in motion, in quiet corners of Kyoto, Amsterdam, Paris and beyond. Some of us are building schools. Others are redesigning jobs. Some are rethinking housing. All of us are looking for a better way forward.

And if we make these shifts, not just in policy but in mindset, we don't just protect our industry.

We elevate it.

CHAPTER THREE

Not present

In this chapter we dive deeply into one of the most urgent cultural shifts affecting hospitality today, the erosion of presence in an age of digital saturation. Through vivid real-world stories, from silent Michelin-starred dining rooms to train journeys drained of human connection, we'll reveal how technology and constant connectivity fragments attention, dulls empathy and quietly dismantles the shared rituals that once defined great hospitality.

Not only this, but technology, for all its benefits, also often actually makes it easier to sidestep the small frictions and connective tissue of social life. Groceries arrive at our doors, meals appear without us leaving our homes and premium travel keeps us at a distance from fellow passengers. These conveniences spare us effort, but at what cost? They help chip away at the everyday encounters that once kept us connected. In subtle ways, we end up "purchasing" ourselves out of relationships, trading them for efficiency and discovering too late the emptiness that follows.

Together these factors present us with one of the central contradictions of modern hospitality; although it is tempting to give people what they appear to want, screens, convenience and insulation from others, what they actually need and what truly nourishes them, is presence and connection. To offer only what is easy risks deepening the problem; to offer what is needed requires courage. In fact, study after study shows that even brief conversations with strangers can lift our mood, far more than scrolling ever does. These human moments, awkward though they may seem at times, are the threads that hold us together.

Beyond this individual level, our obligations to one another, within families, neighbourhoods, even cities, have been hollowed out. Many people no longer know their neighbours, let alone feel bound by a sense of shared community. This erosion of the social fabric leaves guests arriving not just distracted, but often untethered, carrying a quiet loneliness into the very spaces where hospitality could offer repair.

What we face, then, is not just digital distraction but a dismantling of the wider ecosystem that helped sustain community. This isn't a problem hospitality can solve alone; it reflects much larger cultural and structural shifts. But the very fact that the social fabric is fraying makes the role of hospitality more important, not less. Hotels can still stand as places where connection is protected, where attention is valued and where people are gently reminded of what we all most deeply need.

Therefore, throughout this chapter, we challenge hoteliers to see digital distraction not as a failing of our guests, but as a part of a collective condition of the moment and together explore how we can respond with empathy, creativity and cultural leadership. It is both a critique and a call to action. It explores a series of cultural shifts disrupting hospitality, once a sanctuary for rest, connection and transformation, through real-world stories and offers a framework for renewal. It also suggests that hospitality be understood as a two-way exchange. For while the hotelier can create the right conditions, presence cannot be imposed, it requires the guest's participation. Without that buy-in, connection remains elusive.

To navigate this complex situation, we set out a series of essential "mind shifts" which we believe will help the industry reclaim its role as a sanctuary for depth, connection and emotional awakening, in the face of seismic change. Offering practical ways to design spaces, rituals and experiences that invite guests and staff, back into that rarest luxury of all: being connected and fully present.

From Judgement to Collective Compassion: Recognizing Our Shared Condition

Let us begin with what we think is one of the key shifts in perspective that is needed; that we must stop treating digital distractions as a guest problem and begin to see them as a shared human condition. We are all, hospitality staff and guests alike, digital addicts. And like all modern addictions, this one is not simply a matter of willpower or personal habit, it is systemic, rooted in our biology and emotions and deliberately engineered and reinforced by the business models of every major tech company.

Understanding this changes much. It allows us to stop being frustrated and start being empathetic. It helps us design not for an imagined "perfect" guest, but for real, struggling people, guests and team members alike, who are often overwhelmed, overstimulated and not fully aware of what they truly need.

We argue that hospitality must now become a form of care for the digitally fatigued. A place of refuge from hyperstimulation. A quiet but powerful intervention that says: here, you are safe to disconnect, here, you can be human again.

The Roots of a Lack of Focus

Generation Z is the first generation to have fully grown up immersed in constant connectivity. For them and every generation that follows, technology and the internet are not innovations, they are defaults. Fast, fluid and ever-present, digital technology has shaped their entire world. Yet this immersion has come at a cost: an increasing inability to focus or sustain attention.

As Johann Hari explores in Stolen Focus, the consequences of this run deep, affecting not only individuals but also entire industries, including our sector. He argues that we now live in an "attentional pathogenic culture", a society designed to fragment our focus and make deep concentration difficult for everyone, not just the young. We all suffer.

Research supports Hari's concern. One study found that the average American college student switches tasks approximately every 65 seconds. In parallel, University of California professor Gloria Mark observed that adults working in office environments maintain focus on a single task for just three minutes, on average. These findings are echoed across numerous studies: attention spans are shrinking, precisely when demands for critical thinking, creativity and precision are rising. When attention breaks down, so does the ability to solve problems effectively. Mistakes increase. Innovation slows. Creativity suffers. This erosion of cognitive capacity impacts everything, from huge global challenges to the small details of our daily tasks.

In hospitality, the effects are particularly visible. Every guest interaction depends on presence being truly attentive, listening with care and responding with warmth. When attention falters, so does service. As Hari puts it:

> *"Empathy is one of the most complex forms of attention we have, and the most precious. Many of the most important advances in human history have been advances in empathy."*

But empathy cannot thrive without attention. And attention, in today's world, is under siege. Sadly, there are no simple fixes. A weekend digital detox may offer temporary relief, but it does little to address the systemic forces at play. As Hari writes, "It's not your fault you can't focus. It's by design. The truth is that you are living in a system that is pouring acid on your attention every day and then you are being told to blame yourself and to fiddle with your own habits while the world's attention burns."

In an industry already grappling with recruitment and retention challenges, the decline in focus raises urgent questions, firstly:

How can luxury hotels continue to deliver what guests most desire, specifically empathy, personal attention and meaningful human connection?

And just as importantly, how can we, as hoteliers, foster those same values in our teams, so they don't just serve better, but feel better while doing it?

The Disruption of Human Connection

Like so many industries, social media has reshaped the luxury hospitality experience, often not for the better. Today, capturing the moment frequently takes precedence over living it, sometimes at the expense of fellow guests. As long as the experience can be broadcast to the world, enjoying it in real time seems secondary. We've all witnessed many occasions overshadowed by the compulsion to record rather than engage, to consult rather than converse and to isolate rather than socialise. One lunch at an iconic Parisian Palace hotel offers a striking glimpse of how digital habits are reshaping even the most exquisite dining experiences.

Le Meurice: The Silent Spectacle

The Michelin-starred dining room at Hôtel Meurice is a masterpiece of Grand Siècle elegance, crystal chandeliers, Fragonard-style paintings, gleaming marble and refined modern touches by Philippe

Starck. It is breathtaking. In the kitchen, Alain Ducasse's team crafts exquisite dishes, while the front-of-house staff maintains a reputation for excellence.

Yet, on a recent lunch visit, something felt off. It took a moment to understand why: the room was silent. No conversation at the tables. No dialogue between staff and guests. Every table was occupied by one or two diners, each with a phone in hand. Every dish was being meticulously photographed. The real conversations were happening online, not in the room.

What unfolded in the dining room of Le Meurice was more than a quiet lunch; it was a revealing portrait of how our relationship with presence, beauty and hospitality is being redefined by the digital age. That a room of such grandeur, designed to dazzle the senses and encourage refined interaction, could fall into such uncanny stillness is not just notable; it is symptomatic.

Le Meurice is meant to be a stage for life at its most heightened, the crisp choreography of service, the low murmur of conversation, the gleam of silver under crystal light. Its silence was not the stillness of peace, but the hush of disengagement. In a space designed for multisensory immersion, the absence of spoken connection felt dissonant. The dining experience, once defined by intimacy and ritual, had become oddly inert. One could hear the clink of cutlery, but not the warmth of voices.

At the heart of this transformation is an important shift, from participation in the present, to the performance of participation. The presence of a smartphone on every table, positioned, not incidentally, but centrally, signals a significant change in the orientation of attention. The meal, instead of being shared in the moment, was being recorded, edited and offered to an unseen audience elsewhere and everywhere. The primary engagement was not with the people across the table, nor with the room, nor even with the food, but with the projected image of having been there. In this sense, the experience was not lived so much as captured, flattened into content.

Perhaps the most striking part of this event was the lack of the guests' response to the staff. Fine dining is not merely about cuisine; it is a form of theatre in which the service team are key performers, storytellers and interpreters of tradition and artistry. Without that dialogue, this performance collapses. The human touch, the subtle reading of a guest's needs, the rhythm of attention and discretion, the warmth of welcome, becomes muted, if not lost altogether. Screens, it seems, have become both mirror and barrier, reflecting us back to ourselves while shielding us from genuine connection.

Le Meurice is more than a restaurant, it is a sensorial narrative, an embodiment of French history, art and contemporary luxury. But when the space is reduced to a backdrop for photos, its emotional resonance is diminished. Without the intimacy of presence, without attention, even the most stunning setting becomes hollow. The restaurant becomes a gallery, not a gathering.

What this moment at Le Meurice reveals is not just the evolution of dining, but a deeper cultural shift: in an age of hyperconnectivity, presence itself has become a luxury. We seek out rare and beautiful experiences, only to engage with them through a digital intermediary. We travel far to dine in rooms like this, only to step out of them, even while sitting inside. The irony is piercing. The guests came for a once-in-a-lifetime meal. But they leave with only the photos, as precious little is retained of the memory itself. The truest luxury of all, the feeling of being fully there, is quietly set aside.

When Performance Replaces Presence

If Le Meurice illustrates silence born of performance, then Harry's Bar in Venice reveals another form of digital intrusion, this time louder, more disruptive, but equally corrosive to hospitality. What happens when the guest isn't just documenting passively but reshaping the room to suit their personal broadcast?

Harry's Bar in Venice is extraordinary in many ways. Arrigo Cipriani, who began working alongside his father Giuseppe in the 1950s, still makes an appearance at most lunches nearly 70 years later. His presence is electric, he rises to greet every familiar face, which means he is constantly on his feet, recognizing the many regulars. There are few places where the spirit of hospitality feels as alive and personal as it does at Harry's Bar in Venice. And yet, even in such sanctuaries, the modern world seeps in.

On one visit, we watched in dismay as a lady from San Antonio and her companion, both in their early 40s, entered the charming ground-floor dining room. After placing their orders, the woman requested that the waiter give a detailed description of the dishes and asked him to speak loudly and clearly. She was filming and all the attention in the room shifted to her. Once the food arrived, she again took more photos and videos, while her companion quietly ate alone.

This intrusion wasn't just loud in volume, but it was loud in meaning. The woman's request that the waiter describe the dishes loudly shattered the unspoken code that gives Harry's Bar its atmosphere. It wasn't the camera itself that disrupted the room; it was the shift in focus. Where once attention flowed toward the craft of the food, the ritual of service and the unhurried rhythm of the room, now all eyes were pulled toward a single, altogether different performance. In a moment, what was private became public. What was intimate became staged. The atmosphere, built on restraint and mutual respect, faltered under the weight of self-centred spectacle.

At its best, hospitality is a deeply human exchange, a moment of care between guest and host. But in this case, that exchange was co-opted by the lens. The waiter was no longer a partner in a shared experience, but a supporting actor in a scene being scripted for others. This moment captures a larger concern: when the desire to document eclipses the desire to connect, hospitality risks becoming hollow. In these moments, the performance for an unseen audience replaces the ritual occurring between those who are physically present.

Perhaps equally telling amidst this performance was the actions of the influencer's companion, seated silently, eating alone, while the show unfolded around him. Though together at the table, they inhabited different realities, one immersed in the screen, the other relegated to the margins of attention. This subtle disconnect mirrors a broader social trend. In an age of constant digital engagement, physical proximity no longer guarantees emotional presence. Even shared experiences, especially the kind that once created deep personal bonds, can often now unfold in parallel rather than in unison.

There is also, perhaps, a significant and somewhat discordant cultural note beneath this glossy digital surface. Unlike the world of Instagram luxury and the screen, Harry's Bar is the embodiment of old-world European grace, built on discretion, tradition and the unspoken elegance of understatement. The intrusion of filming and self-centred focus felt jarring not just because it was disruptive, but because it collided with the values that the space quietly upholds. In this contrast lies something more than a breach of etiquette, it is a dissonance between two worldviews, one rooted in presence, the other in performance; one built on shared ritual, the other on personal broadcasting. What was once a dialogue is now a monologue.

This was not simply a case of one inconsiderate diner. It was a microcosm of a deeper cultural drift. The erosion of attention, of presence, of intimacy, not through malice, but through the habits of a hyper-connected age.

Whereas guests were once overawed by the experience itself, now the impulse to stage an experience overtakes the desire to live it and thus the essence of hospitality begins to dissolve. The room may look the same, the service may remain impeccable, but the soul of the encounter, the shared humanity at the heart of it, grows ever dimmer. Magic, after all, depends on attention. And when that attention is turned outward, toward a distant and unseen audience, even the most enchanted places can begin to feel ordinary.

The Louvre, Unheard

If the disturbance at Harry's Bar revealed the pitfalls of a certain kind of public performance, then the Louvre offers a subtler, but no less revealing, variation on our theme of the disruption of presence. Here, the performance is internal. Silent. But presence is still fractured.

In the grand halls of the Louvre, a guide pauses mid-sentence, waiting respectfully for a group member to finish with her phone. "Keep going," she says, eyes still on her screen. "I'm listening." It is a phrase we hear often now. It is meant to reassure, but it actually reveals a tension at the heart of modern experience: the widening gap between physical presence and attentional presence. In this case, the woman's body may be in the room, but her focus is split, her attention divided. The words may reach her, but the meaning, most likely, does not land with the same weight. What seems like a small moment, an everyday gesture of multitasking, is, in truth, a telling symbol of how digital habits erode our engagement with the world around us.

The Cost of Divided Attention

Among the marvels of its many achievements, cognitive science has made one thing clear, multitasking dilutes understanding. Human brains simply cannot cope with too many things at once. What this suggests is that even if our group member believes she's "hearing" her guide, her brain is not fully absorbing what's being said. What should be a rich, layered experience, full of history, emotion and visual context, becomes thinner, flatter, more forgettable. The mind skims the surface, but does not dive any deeper than that.

To glance at a screen, even briefly, is to step out of the moment. In that instant, the visitor shifts from participant to passive observer. The Louvre becomes just another backdrop. The room, the guide, the group, all continue, but she is elsewhere, tethered to another reality.

The experience becomes less immersive, less embodied. Less lived. Ultimately a phone, used in the middle of a shared experience, creates an invisible wall. It signals disengagement. However unintentional, it subtly dampens the energy of the group, creating disconnection where there might have been shared curiosity, wonder, or laughter.

This brief scene reminds us that in a world of constant digital reach, attention has become one of the rarest and most precious gifts we can give. To give it fully, even for a few minutes, is to honour the moment, the speaker, our friends and ourselves.

These stories from Le Meurice, Harry's Bar and the Louvre form a constellation. They show not just the individual cost of distraction, but the collective erosion of experience. When one guest disengages, others feel it. The room shifts.

As hoteliers, these are not isolated anecdotes, far from it; instead they are indicators of huge societal shifts. They signal a change in guest behaviour that must be met with cultural awareness, strategic empathy and courageous rethinking of the guest journey.

The Vanishing Journey

So, what happens when the journey itself, once filled with social interaction and reflection, becomes just another moment to be filled with screens? This erosion of presence doesn't only occur in dining rooms and galleries. It also unfolds in transit, where once we found time to think, to connect and to observe.

In the 60s and early 70s, carriages had compartments that seated six to eight people, like small, private sitting rooms. They felt intimate and warm, inviting a certain kind of human connection. When entering a compartment, travellers would often greet everyone with a polite "hello," as though stepping into someone's living room. Small talk would naturally follow, sometimes turning into lively conversations. Life in these compartments operated under a quiet social code, passengers were careful not to disturb others when adjusting a window, seeking fresh air, or pulling down the blind. Travellers expected longer journeys and came prepared. Sharing food was common and it was rare to eat without offering something to fellow passengers. Drinks would follow and soon, what began as a simple meal could become a joyful, communal event. There was a shared sense of responsibility and trust, when someone left the compartment briefly, the others would instinctively watch over their belongings. Beyond the compartment, the corridor offered its own kind of space. Those lingering there were often open to conversation and connections were easy to strike up. Many trains included a dining car complete with white tablecloths, polished silverware, wine lists and a full menu, another space to linger, talk and enjoy the ride.

However, in 1975, French Railways introduced the Corail coach, it featured bus-style seating, no compartments, no doors, no shared intimacy. For some, it was a welcome change; now they could experience freedom from the unspoken etiquette of compartment travel. But with that change, conversation quietly disappeared. Passengers no longer spoke to strangers. They stopped sharing. The train was no longer a social space.

Fast forward to today and the journey from Paris to Marseille now takes just three hours, with trains racing at 300 km/h. The Mediterranean is astonishingly close. Technological progress has delivered air-conditioning, smooth tracks, near silence and onboard Wi-Fi. Most trains now have standard bus-style seating. Occasionally, you'll find two pairs of seats facing each other, these are typically the last to be booked. Few want to sit face-to-face with a stranger. The goal now is simple: arrive as quickly as possible. The journey itself has lost its meaning.

On a recent trip, a young man sat down, took out his tablet, adjusted his earbuds, noted the glare and promptly closed the blind. Half the carriage followed suit. The outside world disappeared. The view, once a highlight of train travel, was now just a distraction.

Three hours passed in silence. No conversation. No scenery. Just digital isolation, uninterrupted. This story of train travel is not simply a meditation on changing transportation. It is, more profoundly, a meditation on the changing texture of human connection, on how space, time and attention have been reconfigured in the digital age.

The Compartment as a Model of Community

These train compartments of the past symbolised a slower, more human rhythm of life. Six to eight strangers sharing a small space naturally created a microcosm of civil society, one where trust, courtesy and conversation were not exceptional but expected. These were spaces where people were not just physically present, but emotionally and socially available. Eye contact led to greetings. Greetings led to talk. Talk often led to relationships, however fleeting.

This model of spontaneous community contrasts sharply with today's digital culture, where face-to-face interaction has been largely displaced by mediated, curated exchanges. What once occurred in real time, with all its unpredictability and vulnerability, now unfolds asynchronously, filtered through screens. The compartment, in this sense, evokes a pre-digital world, tactile, unpredictable and emotionally rich.

In fact, the shift from compartments to Corail-style, bus-like seating was more than a design choice, it was a marker of a broader philosophical and cultural shift. Privacy, once negotiated in a shared space, was now built into the very architecture of the train. And with that came a social withdrawal. No longer required to engage, passengers began to retreat into themselves. The parallels with the rise of social media are striking: both reflect a move from collective participation to personalised curation. Just as travellers avoid sitting face-to-face, social media users increasingly avoid friction, dissent, or uninvited conversation. We customize not just our feeds but our encounters, gravitating toward comfort and predictability over serendipity and surprise.

The young man on the train, tablet out, earbuds in, blind drawn, is not unusual. He is an archetype of contemporary travel, physically present, mentally elsewhere. His gestures are part of a new etiquette of disengagement. Each movement, from selecting content, blocking out light, sealing off sound, reinforces the idea that the journey is not something to be experienced, but something to be endured, optimised, filled. This is not unique to train travel. Across settings, screens have become not just tools but barriers, protecting us from boredom, yes, but also from contact, from difference, from the ambient richness of the world and perhaps above all, from the deep experience one is seeking when traveling.

One of the most subtle losses in this shift is the disappearance of the unexpected. In the days of the compartment, you didn't choose your companions. You had to negotiate differences, to find common ground, to engage across divides. That daily social friction helped cultivate adaptability, empathy and a tolerance for discomfort.

Today, those encounters have largely vanished. We engage when we choose, on platforms that filter and sort for us. What feels like freedom, a combination of choice, control and curation, may in the end be a narrowing of the human experience.

Beneath all this lies a powerful shift in how we relate to time. The older model of train travel embraced slowness. The journey was not just tolerated, it was part of the pleasure. People brought books, newspapers and lunches. They looked out of windows. They watched the landscape pass and watched time unfold. Attention was expansive, not parcelled into 30-second increments. Today, speed and density are the priorities. Every moment must be filled, every gap optimised. Devices turn idle time into productive time, or at least into distraction. But in doing so, they erode something essential: the stillness in which reflection, observation and genuine encounter once occurred.

A Quiet Metaphor for a Noisier World

In this light, the story of the modern train is a quiet metaphor for broader cultural changes. The shift from compartments to individual screens is the story of modern life; a move away from presence, serendipity and depth, toward a fractured experience of time, where distraction, disconnection and constant interruption are the principal features. We are connected, but not together. Surrounded by others, but sealed off in our own digital compartments. Moving faster than ever, but with less and less sense of where we are, or who we are with.

The journey, once a shared experience, is now solitary by design. And in that solitude, something essential is slowly fading.

Navigating the New Reality

These moments raise a critical question: how should luxury hospitality operators navigate this new world? What is at stake here? As hoteliers we are obsessed with delivering 'experiences'. But there is no experience if people are not present.

When social media and screen time take precedence over shared experience and real presence, the essence of hospitality is at risk. In an age of digital intrusion, how can luxury settings preserve their magic, foster connection and maintain the standards that once defined them?

How do we, as hoteliers, give guests what they really want and need, even though, through no fault of their own, they have become digital addicts.

Do Guests Enjoy Themselves More Without Their Phones?

In an age where screens are ever-present, even at the dinner table, a question has emerged in the world of hospitality: *Do guests actually enjoy their meals and outings more when they put their phones away?*

The answer, increasingly, appears to be yes. Whether in restaurants, cafés, or bars, both research and anecdotal feedback suggest that stepping away from the digital world, even briefly, enhances the quality of the experience. Guests often report that conversations feel richer, the atmosphere more memorable and the food more enjoyable. Without the constant pull of notifications or the reflex to document every moment, something subtle but essential is restored, presence. Studies have shown that just having a phone visible on the table can reduce the depth of conversation. When devices are tucked away, people tend to listen more closely, engage more fully and connect more meaningfully. Many guests are surprised by how liberating it feels, not just to disconnect from the digital world, but to reconnect with the real person in front of them, the warmth of candlelight, the echo of shared laughter, the texture of a dish savoured slowly.

Some venues now provide small gestures to encourage this shift: phone baskets, yondr pouches, stickers placed on phone cameras at the entrance of venues, digital detox menus, or even small incentives for going screen-free.[5] What's telling is that even when guests are initially hesitant, most leave feeling more nourished, emotionally as well as physically.

In these moments, it's clear: when the screen disappears, the experience returns. And in that return lies something increasingly rare and increasingly valued. Something luxurious.

Gilberto, A Brazilian Barista In Paris

In a newly gentrified corner of Paris, a small café run by a Brazilian couple has become something unusual. The barista, Gilberto, greets guests with warmth but also with a rule: no laptops. Those who miss the sign soon discover it through Gilberto's easy charm; he points it out with a laugh and a smile that softens what could otherwise feel like a rebuke.

That small gesture changes the rhythm of the place. Without screens, customers notice more: the sounds of the room, the presence of others and, often, Gilberto himself. Conversations begin, sometimes with him and sometimes with strangers who might otherwise have remained invisible behind their devices. What could have been a moment of inconvenience becomes a rare pause in the day, a pocket of calm built around human contact.

Over time, regulars come to see the café as more than a stop for caffeine. Gilberto invites them to tastings, shares stories of his journey and creates an atmosphere that is both intimate and communal. What begins as a small inconvenience, becomes a brief oasis in the middle of each day. It's the calm, the human contact, the rare chance to be fully present. But without Gilberto, his no-laptop policy, his charm and his knack for connection rather than confrontation, none of this happens.

Gilberto's café works because he asks something of his guests; not just to put their laptops away, but to join a shared sense of attention. And by defending attention as something we all share, Gilberto has transformed his café into something more than the usual place to top up one's caffeine levels, it has become a space of connection, something that draws people back time after time.

Annabel's: The Art of Discretion in the Age of Exposure

Annabel's on London's Berkeley Square is more than just a private club, it is a social institution. Founded in 1963 and reimagined in recent years with exquisite maximalist interiors and a global elite membership, the club remains anchored by one defining value: discretion.

In an age where experiences are incessantly photographed, tagged and uploaded, Annabel's stands apart. Phones are not strictly forbidden, but their use is heavily discouraged in many of the club's key spaces. Members know this is a place for presence. There are no influencers live-streaming their cocktails, no flashes interrupting the quiet hum of conversation. It is a throwback, in the most elegant sense, to an era where privacy was a form of luxury and where real life wasn't lived for an audience. Remember, while it can often be tempting in hospitality to simply let guests have what they want, to scroll, to post, to share, this confuses desire with need. What guests and the rest of us, yearn for is connection, presence and moments of unmediated authenticity. What Annabel's demonstrates is that by resisting the pressure to accommodate every surface desire, we can deliver something deeper and far more lasting. Annabel's actually succeeds because it does not simply give people what they say they want; it instead offers what they didn't realise they needed. And crucially, members accept this.

In fact, Annabel's offers a kind of sanctuary. Members speak of it not just as glamorous or exclusive, but as refreshingly unavailable to the outside world. And this is precisely the point. In a city teeming with places to post from, Annabel's is one of the few designed not to be posted at all. The velvet banquettes, the candlelit tables, the garden under a painted sky, all exist not as backdrops for content, but as settings for actual experience, conversation, connection, escape.

In doing so, Annabel's (like Gilberto's Cafe) achieves something we might call protecting the commons of attention. By setting firm standards around distraction, the club guards not just individual experience, but the shared atmosphere in which all its members participate. This is one of the most valuable lessons Annabel's has for hoteliers; that upholding boundaries around presence is not restrictive, but liberating and in doing so it creates the very conditions in which hospitality can flourish.

Ultimately, as the world becomes more connected, clubs like Annabel's remind us that the rarest luxury might now be to disconnect, together.

Hospitality in the Age of Distraction

In this age of digital saturation, emotional disconnection and constant distraction, the true essence of hospitality is quietly under threat. The industry, once rooted in ritual, presence and shared experience, is being reshaped by forces far beyond its control. To reclaim its soul, hospitality must undergo a fundamental transformation. Not through superficial updates or marketing campaigns, but through deep shifts in mindset within individuals, teams and organisations.

What follows are what we believe are the essential mind shifts required for hoteliers and hospitality leaders to meet this cultural moment with clarity, courage and care.

1. From Judgement to Collective Compassion

As mentioned at the beginning of this chapter, we must abandon the notion that digital distraction is simply the failing of our guests. It is not. It is a collective condition, engineered, systemic and shared by every one of us.

Hospitality must therefore evolve into a form of care for the digitally fatigued. We must design not for ideal behaviour, but for real, struggling people. Empathy begins here.

2. From Performance to Presence

Luxury is no longer about spectacle. Guests crave realness, not perfection.

We must shift from performing experiences for a digital audience to being in the moment. Presence, undivided, attentive and human, is now the rarest and most desired luxury of all.

3. From Transactions to Shared Humanity

Hospitality is not a checklist. It is an emotional exchange.

What guests remember is not the folded napkin or the five-star polish, it is being seen, heard and cared for. This shift re-centres the guest journey around empathy and mutual humanity.

4. From Tech-Enhanced to Tech-Conscious Environments

Technology, unexamined, steals attention and intimacy.

We must become stewards of sacred space, spaces where guests can look up, not down. Phone-free rituals, technology-light sanctuaries and digital awareness aren't restrictive, they are restorative.

5. From Instant Gratification to Deep Engagement

Luxury isn't fast. It is slow, layered and thoughtful.

Our role is to invite guests into the richness of unhurried experience, the lingering conversation, the late-night story, the second pot of tea. In these pauses, memory and meaning takes root.

6. From Image to Experience

Today, too many guests come to capture, not to feel.

Let us gently guide them back to the moment. Create atmospheres that quiet the compulsion to perform. Let candlelight, warmth and storytelling invite them to live, not just document, their experiences.

7. From Satisfaction to Awakening

Satisfaction is no longer enough. Guests crave awakening, even if they cannot articulate it.

True hospitality lifts people out of the mundanity we all can often default to. It opens hearts. It nourishes the soul. The deepest gift we can offer is transformation, not just comfort.

8. From Stagecraft to Soulcraft

Hospitality is not theatre. It is a deep, personal practice.

Gone are the days of polished performance alone. What matters now is sincerity, presence and warmth. We must become soulmakers, not stage managers.

9. From Optimization to Reverence

We live in a culture that rushes. But presence cannot be rushed.

The new hospitality honours time, not by managing it, but by elevating it. Creating moments that breathe and inviting guests to slow down, to notice, to feel.

10. From Guest Obsession to Team Empowerment

Exhausted teams cannot offer heartfelt service, so therefore let us not care for our guests alone.

Let us extend our compassion inward. When staff are seen, valued and empowered, they pass that energy on to guests. Presence must be cultivated behind the scenes, too.

These shifts are not easy. But they are necessary.

To reclaim its future, hospitality must become more human, not more perfect. More soulful, not more seamless.

This is the calling: to hold space in a distracted world. To be a sanctuary for depth. To welcome guests not just to our rooms, but to themselves.

Scenario:	**A Rumination on Presence, Emotion and the Reinvention of Luxury**
Setting:	A softly lit, book-lined salon in a restored grand hotel, somewhere between old-world charm and contemporary calm. It's late evening, a fire crackles and there's not a phone in sight.
Characters:	
Elena:	Hotelier and General Manager
Marc:	Tech-savvy entrepreneur in his 50s
Noor:	Gen Z fashion designer

Elena:	Thank you both for agreeing to this. I just want to discuss something that's been on my mind a lot recently, which is basically how do we keep luxury human-centred, in a time where everything is so digital, scalable and optimised?

Marc: Actually, it's funny you say that. I just came from a really great global design summit in Seoul. All the talk was on AI, automation, all that kind of thing, but there were zero and I mean zero, staff experiences. It was honestly weird, as you know what people remember? A doorman who remembers their name. A smile that doesn't feel scripted. All those personal touches.

Noor: Totally. I love tech, but what I think I really want at the moment is a kind of contrast. My last hotel stay was beautiful, but honestly it was totally sterile. I vaguely remember the marble, but I don't really remember the people. It was almost too efficient and frictionless.

Marc: I get that. In my experience seamless is great, but for logistics, right? As for luxury, I think it's more about texture. Those unexpected conversations with a bartender at 11 p.m. It's that kind of thing that makes something unforgettable.

Noor: Yes! It's the same in my industry, luxury isn't just fabric or price. It's the story, the maker, the feeling. People can really sense those things.

Elena: So how do you think we create that here? And not just for guests, but also for teams?

Marc: Purpose? A luxury hotel today isn't just a place, it's a platform. For memory. For emotion. For a pause. If you can design those, you win.

Noor: And make it beautiful. But not perfect. Perfect is cold. People want presence. Spaces that say, "It's okay to be real here."

Elena: *(Smiling)*
Right, I hear that. Actually, we've just launched something called 'The Listening Hour.' There's no service. No menu. Just tea, low light and company. Some people sit in silence. Others talk for the first time that day. I honestly think it feels like a space where people can be way more real than they usually are in the hotel.

Marc: That's smart, almost like a form of emotional UX. It's like you're building rituals, not just rooms.

Noor: Or that you're designing care. I really think that's the new luxury, particularly when everything is moving by so fast and it's difficult to feel that sense of stillness, that sense of being cared for. It can help people feel more themselves and just a little more human.

Travel As Awakening: A Journey Beyond Routine

Throughout this chapter we've seen how digital saturation erodes presence, in dining rooms, cultural landmarks and even in the journeys between them. So to conclude we return to a deeper question at the heart of hospitality: what is travel really for? Beyond the curated images and the checklist of attractions, travel at its best is transformative. It invites us to step out of the everyday, to see with fresh eyes and to reconnect with what is most human in ourselves and others.

Yet this awakening cannot happen if we remain distracted, tethered to our screens. Fundamentally, this is the dilemma we live in, we remain addicted to distraction even as we long to relax. We wrestle with it daily, caught between the tug of immediacy and the hunger for presence and connection.

We can also be tempted to buy our way out of the messiness of a social life that is actually meaningful, with meals delivered instead of shared in restaurants, first-class cabins that insulate us from fellow passengers and apps that replace human contact. But while these options promise convenience, they also strip away the very connections that make life meaningful. We end up paying to avoid one another, only to discover that that very avoidance leaves us emptier in the long run.

The stories we explored in this chapter, from the silent dining room at Le Meurice to the staged performance at Harry's Bar, from fractured attention at the Louvre to the vanishing conversations of train travel, all revealed how this culture of distraction is hollowing out so many experiences that once felt alive. Not only that, but presence, that most essential ingredient of hospitality, is increasingly rare. Yet these examples are not only warnings; they are also reminders of what's at stake. They show us not only the magic that is lost when attention falters but also hint at the possibility of reclaiming it.

Although hospitality alone cannot solve the global forces that fragment attention, it can offer a counterweight. Hospitality becomes, in this sense, a form of care, a refuge from overstimulation, a place where people are invited to slow down, to notice, to feel restored. Hotels, then, must not feed our addiction to distraction, but actually help guests loosen its grip. Their role is then to guide people back to themselves, to offer spaces that quiet the noise rather than amplify it.

And this matters far beyond the walls of a hotel. The forces pulling us apart are not just digital; they extend across our cities and communities. Walkable high streets give way to Amazon deliveries, ghost kitchens and empty storefronts. Public squares are increasingly privately owned, limiting our freedom to gather. Airbnb may bring tourists, but too often it drives out residents and drives up rents, hollowing out neighbourhoods. This can even lead to social housing being sold off, further fraying the social fabric. Taken together these factors are dismantling the very social ecosystem that once held us together. Hospitality cannot reverse these forces alone; but it cannot ignore them either. The more our collective life erodes, the harder it becomes for hospitality to thrive.

So, the question becomes: knowing all this, do we sit back and let it happen, or do we act? Hospitality will never be able to fix every societal fracture. But by choosing to protect attention, to foster connection and to resist the easy path of endless convenience, hoteliers can play a crucial role in countering the tide.

Take heart, there can be a path forward amidst these challenges. Consider especially the "mind shifts" we proposed, moving from performance to presence, from transactions to shared humanity, from optimization to reverence, for these, we believe, are not merely superficial strategies, but actually deep movements in the right direction. Fundamentally they call for a wielding of a kind of courage, in order to deter constant documentation, to create rituals of disconnection, to empower teams as much as guests and to prize sincerity over spectacle. When done with grace, these shifts transform hospitality from an industry of service to something more powerful and deeply human.

This is also where the two-way nature of hospitality becomes clear. Hoteliers also cannot carry even their part of the burden alone. For this presence is a co-created state, depending not only on the host, but also on the guest's willingness to put aside distraction. Crucially, to ask this of guests is actually not a restriction but a gift, for it honours their deeper needs over their passing desires.

For what is travel really for? Not to capture but to connect. Not to optimize but to awaken. At its best, hospitality gives people back to themselves and their deeper needs, at least for the moments of their stay. In a world where distraction has become the default, our calling is clear, to hold space for presence. To remind guests and ourselves, that the rarest luxury is not what can be bought, but what can be felt, being fully, deeply, here.

CHAPTER FOUR

Miswanting

What Guests Think They Want and What They Actually Need

Somewhere, right now, a guest is checking into the hotel of their dreams. The suite is perfect. The marble glows. The curtains billow softly, as if summoned from the pages of a lifestyle magazine. There's a welcome letter, handwritten in impeccable script. A single orchid leans toward the light. Everything is exactly as promised. And yet, within minutes, something begins to feel off.

Maybe it's the silence. Maybe it's the smell of a diffuser that reminds them of another place. Maybe it's just that the view, despite being panoramic and wildly expensive, is still… just a view.

They sip the welcome drink. Smile politely. And quietly wonder:

"Is this it?"

It's not a crisis. It's not even disappointment, really. It's just a soft confusion that sits behind the eyes. Everything they wanted is here. So why doesn't it feel the way they expected?

This chapter is about that subtle ache. That misalignment between what we chase and what actually fulfils. A paradox at the heart of modern luxury hospitality; that guests often pursue experiences they believe will make them happy, yet leave feeling unchanged. And this is where one of the central, counterintuitive insights of this chapter emerges, that true luxury is not about giving guests exactly what they ask for, at least not in the superficial sense. The challenge and the opportunity, is to see beyond those surface desires and sometimes even to withhold them, so that guests can experience what they truly need. In other words, luxury is not the art of indulging every wish, but the art of guiding people past what they think they want, towards deeper satisfactions that create lasting fulfilment. It's not simple. It's a challenge.

Throughout the chapter we'll draw on research in psychology to examine how status symbols, social comparison and social media all amplify this challenge and explore why an endless chase for novelty fails to deliver lasting fulfilment. Through case studies, stories and data, we make the case for hoteliers to initiate a strategic reorientation, turning away from an arms race of material excess and toward experiences that cultivate presence, connection and emotional resonance.

We'll begin by exploring different facets of miswanting, the human tendency to want things that we mistakenly believe will make us happy. But this doesn't mean that people want the wrong things because they're foolish. Rather, it reflects a deeper truth: we are all misled by flawed emotional forecasting, challenging cultural messages, non-stop advertising and some unfortunate evolutionary flaws of the human brain.

Fundamentally, this chapter isn't about correcting or judging. It's about seeing. Understanding. And gently refocusing to offer hospitality that's truthful, deeper and that endures. To help translate these insights into practice, we'll end this chapter by proposing ten "mind shifts" for the human-centred hotelier, shifts from surface desire to deeper need, from spectacle to sanctuary, from performance to presence, that together sketch a roadmap for a more meaningful future of luxury.

The Forecasting Error: When Anticipation Overpromises

It's perhaps unsurprising, but guests often arrive with inflated expectations. Like guests, we all can believe that a particular suite, a meal, or setting will bring us deep and lasting joy. But research shows that that kind joy is often fleeting as we consistently overestimate how good things will feel once we get them.

We owe this understanding to psychologists Daniel Gilbert and Timothy Wilson, who studied a phenomenon they called affective forecasting, that is, our ability to predict how future events will make us feel. In one of their most revealing studies, Gilbert and his colleagues looked at a group of university professors awaiting a tenure decision. Faculty members anticipated that receiving tenure would bring them great, sustained happiness and that conversely being denied tenure would plunge them into long-term disappointment. Yet, when researchers followed up months and years later, both groups had returned to remarkably similar levels of happiness. The event that once loomed so large had faded into the background of daily emotional life.

But this phenomenon is not confined to university professors, as a similar pattern emerged in Gilbert and Wilson's study of social exclusion. College students were told they were either accepted into an exclusive group or rejected. Predictably, those left out initially felt disappointed, but within a few weeks, their happiness had rebounded.

The lesson from their research was clear, people overestimate the intensity and duration of future emotions, both positive and negative. We think winning the lottery (or going on a dream holiday) will change everything. We think failure will ruin us. But in reality, we're surprisingly emotionally resilient, and poor predictors of what will truly bring lasting joy. In essence, because our emotional forecasts are flawed, we often chase experiences, possessions, or milestones that don't deliver the fulfilment we imagined. In luxury hospitality, this means that guests may arrive craving the spectacular, only to find that what lingers in memory are the subtler, more human touches they never thought to ask for.

This tendency to misjudge the impact of future joys and sorrows connects directly to another psychological pattern, hedonic adaptation, which explains why even when our forecasts come true, the emotional payoff rarely lasts for long.

Hedonic Adaptation: Why Pleasure Diminishes

In 1978, psychologists Philip Brickman, Dan Coates and Ronnie Janoff-Bulman conducted one of the most famous studies on happiness and adaptation. They compared two extreme life experiences: winning the lottery and becoming paraplegic. Initially, lottery winners reported a temporary surge in happiness, while paraplegics experienced emotional loss. But astonishingly, one year later, both groups had returned to a baseline level of happiness similar to that of the general population. In both directions, people had emotionally adapted to their new realities. This phenomenon, known as hedonic adaptation, means that our emotional system tends to normalise whatever it encounters. New possessions, exciting events (or experiences), even crushing setbacks quickly lose their emotional charge. In other words, the best things in life don't feel good for long and even terrible events are rarely as ruinous as we predict. And yet, we spend much of our lives striving for things that only offer a brief emotional bump.

In our industry stories like this abound. Take guests on their lifetime holiday in Tanzania, they are over-excited by the view of thousands of wildebeests during migration in the morning of day one. When the ranger points out wildebeests on the last day of the safari, at best, they nod... Or one of our guests at a Paris hotel, a couple who had just sold their business. They decided it was time to enjoy themselves and set a few goals: they would build USA's most expensive house and she would be 'Haute Couture's' best customer. They succeeded in reaching both goals. They would come to Paris for years staying in the city's most expensive suites. For their home, they bought the rarest and most expensive 18th century French furniture. Their house had to look as grand as Versailles. It did. Then they went on to buy a ranch, a house in Ibiza, another one in Courchevel... It never stopped.

When all is said and done, no matter how wealthy you are, you cannot escape hedonic adaptation, just like the rest, you're stuck on that treadmill. Not only that, but as our emotional systems quickly normalise both triumph and tragedy, then the kinds of goals we pursue become even more critical, but too often, those goals are set by a culture that teaches us to chase objects, status and spectacle rather than meaning.

Mistaken Materialism: Why Chasing Objects Doesn't Lead to Happiness

Here we turn to Tim Kasser, one of the leading voices in the psychology of values and well-being. His research explores what we are taught to want in the first place and why those desires so often steer us away from genuine fulfilment. In his work, Kasser, along with colleagues Richard Ryan and Edward Deci, developed the Aspiration Index, a research tool that helps researchers and their subjects classify life goals as either intrinsic (like close relationships, personal growth and community involvement) or extrinsic (such as wealth, fame and image or status).

Using this tool across numerous studies involving thousands of participants, the researchers uncovered findings that were consistent and troubling: that those who prioritised extrinsic goals reported lower life satisfaction, higher levels of anxiety and depression and weaker interpersonal relationships. Even when people successfully attained those external goals, they usually found themselves less fulfilled than they expected. In a series of follow-up studies, Kasser extended his research to children and adolescents, revealing that young people raised in highly materialistic environments, where consumerism and social comparison were central, were more likely to suffer from emotional distress, lower self-esteem and disconnection. Taken together, these studies point to a major driver of miswanting: we are taught by society to want things that actively make us less happy.

Recognising this deeper truth forces us to confront a hard question: if so much of what guests think they want won't actually make them happy, what should hotels continue to invest in and should they rethink their approach entirely? Take city spas, for instance. In London, luxury hotels compete fiercely to outdo each other in spa offerings. Recently, a leading London hotel in Belgravia launched an 18,000 square foot spa, at a cost of many millions. The usage rate by hotel guests? Just 4%. For a 100-room hotel, that equates to an average of six guests per day when fully booked. At an equally luxurious hotel nearby in Knightsbridge, complete with a 25-metre pool, the guest usage rate is just 5%.

In Paris meanwhile, top-tier hotels have raced to secure three Michelin stars, Le Bristol, Plaza Athénée, George V and Le Meurice among them, while most of the others boast at least two. Yet the usage rate of these restaurants by hotel guests is between 2 and 3%. Hotel guests largely don't go. The restaurants are rarely profitable. Yet hotels lean heavily on their star chefs for positioning and marketing, despite this being a feature guests largely ignore.

Isn't that odd?

Perhaps not so odd when we remember that guests' needs were never about square footage or star ratings, they were about feeling cared for, at ease and connected. For if hoteliers respond to every request without pausing to reflect, they can risk missing the bigger picture. Just as with children, constant indulgence doesn't always lead to greater happiness. What makes the real difference is seeking a deeper understanding of what guests truly need, going beyond surface requests to uncover the experiences and feelings that create lasting satisfaction.

What Luxury Really Means Now

Understanding those deeper needs requires taking a moment to examine how our very idea of 'luxury' has evolved and why simply adding more and apparently better things has never guaranteed happier guests. In fact, in the modern hospitality landscape, if you still see the luxury market as an arms race to offer ever-nicer material goods, not only will you not win, it may in fact mean you've misunderstood the game entirely.

But to understand this 'game', let us turn to a key moment in our modern understanding of luxury; when the term 'jet-set' was coined by a reporter for the New York American Journal, one Igor Cassini. At the time, this term described only those 'A-listers' who were the ones wealthy enough to travel by jet. The term really took off in 1958 with the launch of Boeing's 707 jet engine airplane, which travelled on the Pan Am route from New York to London.

For the next 50 years, aspirational B-listers would try to follow in their footsteps and as airlines, especially in First and Business class constantly tried to up the ante, hotels also found themselves concentrating on elevating their service to levels never reached before.

Consider a luxury hotel room from the 1950s: a black-and-white TV, a colourful bedspread and a rotary phone connected to an operator. By the 1960s, the first colour televisions were introduced, costing per set £300 at that time, around £5,600 in today's money.

Now compare that to a hotel room today: Wi-Fi, streaming services, a global TV catalogue, a high-tech large screen TV, 1,000-thread-count sheets, central temperature control, sophisticated lighting systems, marble bathrooms, curated minibars with accompanying pantries stuffed full of a dizzying array of treats and much, much, more. These two rooms seem worlds apart. And yet, there's little compelling evidence that guest satisfaction has increased in proportion to the rise in product offering.

Why?

Because, as we explored earlier, impressive material goods do not reliably lead to happiness. We adapt. Quickly. This is the fundamental psychological challenge of hedonic adaptation. Crucially, the relentless pursuit of ever-better 'stuff' hasn't just failed to make us happier, it has also blinded many of us hoteliers to the simple truth that what guests most long for today isn't more stuff, but more connection. It's only when needs like this are addressed directly that luxury feels truly meaningful.

The Futility of the Arms Race

All this means that if we want luxury to have a more profound impact, better meeting the deeper needs of our guests, we must stop competing on material signifiers alone. In fact, in luxury hospitality, especially when serving ultra-high-net-worth individuals, it's especially futile. Until relatively recently, hotels were more beautiful and better equipped than the houses of their guests. But today, these guests often have multiple residences with world-class finishes, custom-built amenities and staff-to-guest ratios that few hotels could match. Trying to impress them with sheer material abundance is not only wasteful and nigh on impossible, it misses the point entirely.

In fact, this fixation on abundance is not limited to hospitality, it reflects a wider cultural shift toward expecting perfection in every product and service, a shift that has reshaped how we consume and how easily we become dissatisfied. We have become such experts at producing whatever we need so efficiently, so productively, that we are used to near perfection. Anything less and we start to complain.

You order a laptop on the internet and it is delivered the next day in a perfectly packed box. You take everything out of the box, plug in the computer, switch it on and… it works. That computer has been assembled with parts originating from countries spread across the globe and handled by people of different nationalities, faiths, genders and ages. Some of the components are engineered to a precision of 14 nanometres. The parcel has passed all the red tape of border controls and import duties and it arrives on your doorstep, just 24 hours after you order it, working to perfection. Yet we think nothing of it.

In fact, despite expending vast amounts of energy across the world on producing such 'perfect' products, people in ageing-economies are generally less happy than they were 50 years ago, before any of this advanced 'stuff' existed.

HAS ECONOMIC GROWTH ADVANCED HUMAN MORALE?

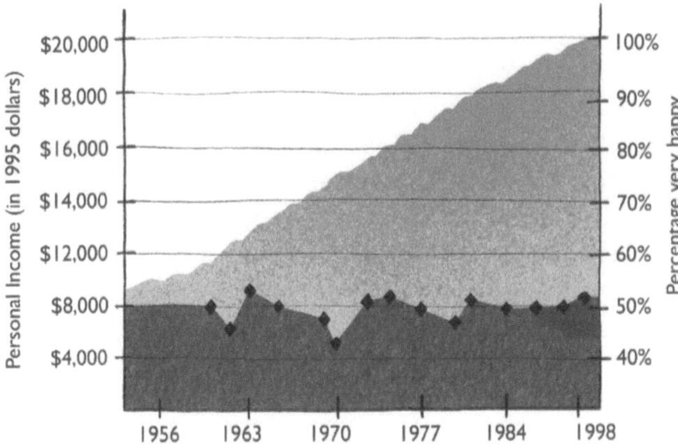

NOTE: While inflation-adjusted income has risen, self-reported happiness has remained relatively flat. Income data from the US Commerce Department, Bureaus (1975), and Economic Indicatiors. Happiness data from General Social Surveys, National Opinion Research Center, University of Chicago.

Source: David G. Myers, "The Funds, Friends, and Faith of Happy People", published in 2000

We find the same phenomena in our sector. Luxury hotels today are fully furnished with the latest 'stuff', decorated by world-renowned designers, covered with the finest materials, and yet hotel guests think this is completely normal and, in fact, to be expected. But revealingly what is not so normal any more is to have great, personal relationships with hotel staff; and yet that connection, that atmosphere, that warmth is what most clients crave. Fundamentally, while clients may come for the hotel, they return for the relationships.

Smart Investing for Fulfilment

But here's the tension: although material goods don't make guests happy, sub-par goods will disappoint. Although we'll explore this in more depth later, here's the guiding principle:

Material must be "good enough" – no more, no less.

It should never distract. But it must never disappoint.

What defines "good enough" will depend on the guest's reference points, what they're used to in their personal life. For some, it may be a private jet. For others, the elegance of simplicity. This means that knowing our guests, the way they live, work and play, becomes more critical than ever before if we are to make the right investment decisions. What is essential is directing our greatest investments toward staff and experience design, the elements that science and positive psychology consistently show bring lasting guest happiness. Because, ultimately, luxury is not about what we display, but about how guests feel when they can stop performing and simply be themselves.

Extreme Individualism: Societal and Technological Shifts

If investing wisely means shifting focus from material display to human experience, then the next challenge is understanding why, in a world of unprecedented connectivity, people so often overlook the very interactions that could bring them the most joy. In fact, even brief, low-stakes interactions can contribute powerfully to our sense of belonging and happiness and yet, as research shows, we often underestimate their value and choose isolation instead.

Nicholas Epley, a behavioural scientist at the University of Chicago Booth School of Business, is a great example of a researcher exploring this specific problem. He conducted a series of experiments in Chicago to explore the psychological effects of engaging with strangers during daily commutes on suburban trains. These studies[6] revealed that commuters who initiated conversations with strangers experienced more positive and enjoyable commutes in comparison to those who remained silent or followed their usual routines. Interestingly, participants initially predicted that engaging with strangers would be less pleasant and more unproductive than solitude. However, their actual experiences contradicted these expectations, indicating a common misjudgement about the benefits of social interactions with strangers.

Further experiments extended these findings beyond trains to buses, taxis and also laboratory settings, consistently showing that social engagement led to more positive experiences. The research also identified a key reason for people's reluctance to initiate conversations, the assumption that others are not interested in connecting. In reality, most individuals are open to such interactions, suggesting that this belief is a significant barrier to social engagement. These insights have practical implications, especially in urban environments where people often experience isolation despite being surrounded by others.

Despite Epley's research being conducted in Chicago, the CTA (Chicago Transport Authority) never announced any initiatives or changes aimed at encouraging such interactions on their trains. In contrast, the study's replication in the United Kingdom, in collaboration with the BBC, led to initiatives like "Crossing Divides on the Move Day."

Crossing Divides on the Move Day was a UK-wide initiative launched by the BBC on 14 June 2019 as part of its broader Crossing Divides season, which aimed to bridge social and political divides through storytelling and community engagement. The initiative focused on encouraging conversations among strangers on public transport, to enhance well-being and reduce feelings of loneliness.

Key features of the initiative included Virgin Trains designating Coach C on its West Coast services as a "chat carriage," inviting passengers to engage in conversations with fellow travellers, while Arriva Buses distributed "conversation starter" cards across England, Wales and Scotland to prompt interactions among passengers. As for National Express, they employed actors and poets on Birmingham's Route 11 to initiate dialogues and performances that encouraged passenger engagement and Translink in Northern Ireland promoted cross-community conversations on the Glider service connecting East and West Belfast.

All these initiatives sought to challenge the common tendency of commuters to remain isolated during journeys, often absorbed in personal devices. By facilitating opportunities for spontaneous conversations, the campaign aimed to create a greater sense of belonging and community among passengers. Feedback from participants indicated that these interactions often led to more enjoyable and meaningful travel experiences, aligning with Epley's findings that engaging with strangers can positively impact mood and social connectedness.

While the campaign was met with enthusiasm by many, it also acknowledged that not all passengers might be comfortable with such interactions, emphasizing that participation was entirely voluntary. Overall, Crossing Divides highlighted the potential for simple, everyday interactions to bridge social gaps and combat loneliness in public spaces.

But these everyday personal choices, to connect or to retreat, don't just shape the lives of individuals; they instead reflect deeper socio-cultural currents, which is why understanding the rise of individualism is so critical for hoteliers seeking to grasp what truly drives the guest experience today.

Individualism and the Rise of the One-Person Household

To more clearly understand the factors involved in this broad move towards individualism, we must revisit the work of Geert Hofstede, one of the founding figures of intercultural psychology. In the late 1960s, Hofstede, then Director of Human Resources at IBM, conducted one of the most ambitious global workforce surveys ever undertaken. From this data, he identified four primary dimensions of cultural difference. Perhaps the most consequential for luxury hoteliers is the Individualism–Collectivism spectrum.

In this model individualistic cultures value personal autonomy, self-fulfilment and independence from extended family and social groups. Here, identity is defined by "I" rather than "we." Decisions are guided by personal benefit and self-expression, rather than group harmony or traditional expectations.

By contrast, collectivist cultures emphasise loyalty, interdependence and the well-being of the group over individual preference. Identity is rooted in family, community and shared responsibility, with decisions often shaped by consensus, tradition and the desire to maintain social harmony. Research on the dynamics of the Individualism–Collectivism spectrum seems to suggest that as countries grow richer, they tend to become more individualistic. With data going back to the 70s, this evolution is observable today in rising economies across the Global South; as material prosperity increases, so does individualism. Yet alongside this trend sits a mistaken assumption: that greater individualism automatically translates into greater happiness, when in fact research consistently shows that excessive individualism often erodes social connections, leaving people more isolated rather than fulfilled. As this suggests, one consequence of this global drift toward individualism is a diminishing familiarity with the daily negotiations and compromises that community requires. As communal obligations recede, so too do the skills and patience, needed to navigate them. And it's not just that. Surrounded by the increasing wealth and development of our societies we need each other a lot less for the daily material aspects of life. We can survive after a fashion without our neighbours. We don't rely on our co-villagers for safety and security. We don't need each other to harvest. But this survival is not a fulfilling form of life.

But let's face it, it often feels easier to be silent than to engage with a stranger. Whatever the emotional outcome is. Engaging takes more than a little bit of courage and the kind of mental head space that not everyone has after a long day at work. So sharing, be it at home, with the family, the neighbourhood, can be tough. It requires negotiation, diplomacy, frustration and a good dose of compromise. When sharing a home, everyone in the household has tasks to do, responsibilities and must adhere to unwritten house rules. For example, if grandmother lives at home, it means looking after her rather than spending time doing something that seems more satisfying.

And yet, it is precisely in these moments, of tending to a grandmother, negotiating with siblings, or sacrificing one's immediate comfort, that the richest forms of happiness often take root. Unlike the fleeting ease of effortlessness, the meaning that comes from giving and sustaining others endures, not in spite of the friction it involves, but often because of it. In fact, research in psychology consistently shows that the most satisfying pleasures are those tied to contribution, care and belonging. Luxury hoteliers should remember this truth and although transcendent moments in the hot tub may dazzle in the instant, it is the harder, more relational pleasures, the ones that ask something of us (and of our guests), that leave the deeper imprint.

So while being alone can feel like the easier route, over time, these decisions can have major downsides that conversely help demonstrate how much we actually need each other, not only for our own wellness, but for the success of our societies. Not only that, but as these everyday bonds of interdependence fade, what often fills the void is not ease or contentment, but a creeping loneliness that casts a shadow over even the wealthiest and the 'freest' among us.

Loneliness: The Silent Companion of Wealth

The most individualistic country on Hofstede's index is the United States, a nation celebrated for its apparent personal freedoms and entrepreneurial zeal. It is also, perhaps not coincidentally, one of the most chronically lonely. Research consistently links individualistic societies with higher rates of social isolation, mental health concerns and a craving for meaningful connection. What begins as autonomy can turn into disconnection. In such environments, the pursuit of private success often replaces communal belonging.

This shift toward individualism is not just a matter of personal feeling, it also shapes how households and even communities form and function. As social bonds loosen, living arrangements shift, reflecting a broader move toward independence and separation in daily life. More than ever before people live alone and even those who share a home often live parallel lives. Individualism within families and homes has also been made easier thanks to hundreds of devices that allow everyone in the household to do their own thing if they so wish. In the 1950's, everyone would gather at the movies, the sole place to watch a film. With the advent of TV's, families stayed home to watch programmes together, while today, every household member tunes into their own series, in their own time. These monumental shifts have also taken place incredibly rapidly, in just a few generations.

Ultimately, individualism is not a one-dimensional story. On the one hand, it has opened up extraordinary freedoms, such as the liberty to choose our careers, our beliefs, our partners and even our faiths. These are not just consumer choices, but deep civic and personal freedoms that would have been unimaginable in more conformist, oppressive cultures of the past. On the other hand, in its most modern forms, individualism has created new challenges. The same technologies that extend personal liberty also risk isolating us, substituting screens for face-to-face contact, weakening bonds of community and normalising disconnection. It is tempting to celebrate each step further toward autonomy as "progress." And in many respects, compared to rigid traditional systems, it is. But taken to an extreme, this trajectory leads to atomisation, a kind of liberty that hollows itself out, eroding the very social fabric we depend on.

True progress, then, is not about moving endlessly in one direction, but about balancing freedom with connection. This hollowing of connection in an age of rising individualism is not happening in isolation, it is being powerfully accelerated by digital platforms that shape not only how we connect, but also what we think we desire. This is where we believe hospitality can play a unique role: hotels can be rare spaces that preserve individual freedom while actively cultivating genuine human connection.

Chasing Dopamine Instead of Meaning

This rise in individualism doesn't exist in a vacuum. It's playing out in a world where digital platforms shape not only how we live, but also what we think we want, often exacerbating this lonely shift. By curating endless highlight reels of other people's lives, they don't just reflect our desires, they help create them. This is where psychology offers an important lens; research by Martin Seligman and Tim Kasser shows that two forces, affective-forecasting errors and status-driven social comparison, mislead people about what will truly bring lasting fulfilment. Social media has become the perfect delivery system for both biases, with TikTok and Instagram now acting as global, always-on amplifiers for both forces, super-charging miswanting in ways earlier media never could. The result is a constant feed of seductive but incomplete snapshots, designed to keep us scrolling while subtly warping our expectations of what real happiness looks like.

Fundamentally much of what these platforms present are perfect vignettes stripped of context, a 15-second room tour, a plunge-pool breakfast, a cliffside infinity bath, while cropping out the jet-lag, the crowds, the hassle and the cost. This means that viewers over-estimate how much joy a similar experience would bring, falling neatly into the affective-forecasting trap described by Gilbert and Wilson. The effect is reinforced by reward loops, as TikTok's "For You" feed and Instagram's Explore page quickly learn which images and videos spike your dopamine, serving you ever shinier iterations of these templates. The scale is staggering, TikTok now counts roughly 1.6 billion monthly active users, each one feeding the loop. Yet algorithms don't satisfy a need, it can only inflame a want. The distinction matters deeply for hoteliers.

These platforms also function as planet-wide comparison engines. Remember that while Tim Kasser's work shows that extrinsic goals erode well-being, social media actually hugely inflates our reference group from "people I know" to "people richer, prettier, or luckier than I'll ever meet." Not only that, but as popularity is quantified in likes, follows, views and comments, this turns status into a number you can track and compare, at a glance; a series of curated lives that set a bar that no one individual can live up to. Unsurprisingly, studies consistently link heavy Instagram use, upward comparison and depressive symptoms, with the most passive scrollers feeling the worst.

The travel industry has been quick to adapt to this environment. Once reliant on glossy brochures, marketers now know that a single viral reel can rewrite a destination's demand curve overnight. Research by Expedia finds that two-thirds of travellers choose a hotel partly because of social-media images and in the luxury segment, Right Metric's 2023 audit shows that pool-deck drone shots, cliff-edge bathtubs and designer-label breakfast trays drive the highest engagement. The result is a self-perpetuating loop: a user sees an aspirational clip, books the hotel for the photo-op, posts their own version and the algorithm serves it to the next guest. Miswanting spreads virally, while hoteliers feel pressure to create ever more "Instagrammable" spectacles that may do little to improve authentic fulfilment.

All of this plays into what Dr Anna Lembke calls the "dopamine nation" as short-form content deliver micro-rewards at extraordinary speed (TikTok users swipe every six seconds on average) and each swipe resets the pleasure set-point, Kasser's hedonic treadmill in fast forward. Meanwhile, influencers blur the line between lifestyle and advertising. A *#gifted* stay pairs the fantasy of belonging with a booking link, monetising miswanting in real time. Guests arrive primed to tick extrinsic boxes, the shot, the tag, the brag, rather than seek intrinsic pleasures like connection, mastery, or meaning.

But not all pleasures are equal. Some are fleeting jolts of dopamine, delightful in the moment, but gone almost as soon as they arrive. Others endure, leaving a residue of meaning that guests carry long after check-out. Luxury hospitality should aspire to offer the latter: experiences that compound in memory, a "savings account" rather than a "current account". Not the easy come, easy go, of a micro-reward, but rather something that lingers longer in the soul.

Social Comparison: When Status Overshadows Connection

If social media lures us with fleeting dopamine hits, then social comparison ensures we stay hooked, turning travel, lifestyle and even success itself into competitions measured not by meaning, but by status. As we discussed earlier, although it is Hedonic adaptation that explains why the thrill of even the grandest experiences fades and why we continue to chase still more, one of the forces that can keep us locked on that treadmill is social comparison. This is the process of measuring our worth not by how we feel, but by how we stack up against others. It's a challenge we are sure we're nearly all familiar with, the problem of always comparing ourselves, whether to our friends, neighbours, family, colleagues or even strangers. We want what they have and we aspire to be who they are, often without stopping to consider how it actually makes us feel.

Comparison gets even trickier when we make unrealistic social comparisons with actors on TV, with social media influencers, with models in magazines, people we only have a parasocial relationship with and who may be living very different material lives. When we compare ourselves in this way, consciously or unconsciously, not only can it leave us feeling wanting (in the sense of being insufficient), but it actually makes us feel wanting.

Economist and psychologist Robert H. Frank explored an almost disturbing aspect of this effect in a compelling experiment. Participants were asked to choose between two hypothetical scenarios: in one earning $50,000 a year while everyone around them earned $25,000 and in the other earning $100,000 a year while others earned $200,000. The results were striking. Most people preferred the lower income, provided it meant they were better off relatively. The absolute increase in comfort and lifestyle mattered less than their standing in the social hierarchy. This preference reveals how (mis-)wanting is often driven by status anxiety, not real need. We desire things that elevate us above others, not necessarily things that improve our well-being.

And so, while social comparison keeps us grasping at status, it also reveals the emptiness of that pursuit, setting the stage for a deeper question: what kinds of happiness actually endure?

The Fix: From Shallow Happiness to Meaningful Contentment

It seems chasing status rarely delivers what we're really after. The satisfaction it brings is shallow and short-lived, leaving us still searching for something deeper. So, what's the solution? It's "something" that isn't found in comparison, but rather is rooted in the kinds of experiences and connections that genuinely nourish us. Here we turn to Martin Seligman, often considered the founder of positive psychology, whose work challenged traditional views of happiness as mere pleasure. In fact, to counter this flawed understanding he introduced a model of flourishing based on five pillars: Positive emotion, Engagement, Relationships, Meaning and Accomplishment, known as the PERMA model.

His research showed that intrinsically meaningful activities create more durable happiness than fleeting pleasures. For example, in one well-known experiment, participants were asked to write and deliver a "gratitude letter" to someone in their life they had never properly thanked. The act of reflecting, expressing appreciation and sharing it sparked not only a surge of positive emotion in the moment, but a significant and lasting boost in happiness greater than that from simply indulging in pleasurable activities.

Another study focused on character strengths, the core traits such as curiosity, kindness, or bravery that shape how we engage with the world. Participants were guided to identify their top strengths and then use one of them in a novel way each day for a week. Something as simple as applying creativity to solve a small problem, or showing kindness in an unexpected setting, proved remarkably powerful, as this simple, strengths-based intervention led to elevated happiness for up to six months. Together these findings reinforce a key central insight, we often miswant because we (unconsciously) neglect what truly sustains us, including relationships, growth, purpose and engagement.

If positive psychology reminds us what truly sustains happiness, the next challenge is seeing how these insights play out in the real world, a world where social media has reshaped not only our desires, but the entire marketplace that caters to them. Fundamentally the mechanics of social media platforms don't just influence individual desires, they actively rewire the marketplace, shaping both what guests expect and what hoteliers feel compelled to deliver. In this sense TikTok and Instagram have transformed miswanting from a cognitive bias into a business ecosystem. For luxury properties, the question is no longer whether guests arrive with distorted expectations, they do. But rather the opportunity is to convert that performative desire into authentic fulfilment.

Implications for Luxury Hoteliers

Miswanting Driver	Social-Media Amplifier	Strategic Counter-Move
Forecasting error	Idealised micro-videos	Expectation management. Show unfiltered behind-the-scenes stories; brief guests honestly pre-arrival, play up the beauty of real and/or unexpected things.
Hedonic adaptation	Endless feed of newer, cooler hotels	Curate novelty with narrative and variety. Rotate pop-up residencies (chefs, artists) that tell a continuing story so return visits feel fresh yet meaningful.
Mistaken Materialism	Showing off the "stuff" in the hotel, boasting of "more" stuff from food to wine to fancier decor	Emphasise the Experiences. Show what it's like to be there emotionally and psychologically, from interesting conversations to unusual bits of history.
Individualism	Solo scrolling in-room	Engineer connection. Host micro-events (sunset mixology for six guests, communal chef's table) and nudge participation via opt-in chat groups.

Miswanting Driver	Social-Media Amplifier	Strategic Counter-Move
Chasing Dopamine, Not Meaning	Promising bliss, focusing on the "Instagramability" of the space	Promising meaningful connection, focusing on what a guest might do in the hotel to improve their life, from having a meaningful routine to a meaningful conversation
Status comparison	Visible like-counts, influencer stays	Re-frame status. Spotlight purpose-driven initiatives (local conservation, craft), turning acclaim toward contribution rather than ostentation.

As this table makes clear, the solution to all these problems is to design the kinds of experiences, for example, an artist residency, that photograph well but live even better, rewarding guests not just with views, but with value that endures after the post is forgotten. Do that and your hotel becomes more than a backdrop for social media; it becomes that rare place where the promise of luxury and the psychology of happiness finally align.

Designing for the Soul, Not Just the Senses

This shift, from chasing likes to cultivating lasting meaning, points us toward the next horizon: designing not just for the senses, but for the soul. For as we peel back the layers of luxury, a deeper truth emerges: guests are not merely in search of indulgence, they are in search of meaning. But finding the route that leads there is not straightforward, as guests so often arrive with unrealistic expectations.

As we have discussed throughout this chapter, miswanting reminds us that the shine of marble, the scarcity value of wine, or the size of a suite may not deliver what guests truly crave. The greatest gift luxury can offer is not a thing, but a feeling, the sense of being understood, uplifted and genuinely connected. The future of luxury hospitality therefore lies not in grander design or rarer commodities, but in a shift of intent: from impressing to enriching, from delivering to elevating, from transacting to transforming.

True hospitality, we thus argue, must ultimately be about guiding guests toward what they truly need. It's time for hoteliers to become architects of fulfilment, weaving in moments of resonance, fostering spaces for real connection and gently steering guests toward experiences that nourish their deeper selves.

When we accept that true currency of luxury is not gold, but belonging, purpose and emotional richness, we may begin to move from service to stewardship and from comfort to well-being that lingers long after checkout.

Scenario:	**The Table for Four, A Conversation on Miswanting**
Setting:	A private salon overlooking Lake Geneva. Clean lines, natural materials and a quiet dignity. A single round table, linen laid simply, a candle flickering between four figures.
Characters:	
Jonas:	General Manager, late 30s, thoughtful and ambitious, reshaping his hotel's culture from within.
Jay:	Gen Z tech entrepreneur, brilliant, restless, always scanning for what's next.
Sage:	Vegan American millionaire in his 60s, serene, introspective, former finance titan turned advocate for mindful living.
Hervé:	CEO, mid-40s, mission-driven, leading a hospitality group committed to sustainability and social impact.

Jonas	*(Raising his glass):* Here's to the quiet things that matter and to remembering what we often forget we really want.
Hervé:	I'll drink to that. Honestly, we spend so much time building what guests ask for, but I wonder if we should be designing for what they really need.
Jay:	*(Grinning)* You mean after they've already posted the room tour selfies and moved on to the next bit of 'content' creation?
Sage:	*(Chuckles)* Frankly, I've been that guy. Had the yacht, the villa, the private chef, the whole thing. And it's impressive, sure, at least for a while, but it's not all that meaningful. To be honest, that's often just noise and the stuff that sticks with me is quieter and a little smaller, times with friends, that kind of thing.
Jonas:	I've been thinking about this whole… not, situation exactly… but conundrum, I suppose? I guess it comes down to this question, what if our real job as hoteliers is not just providing the space for that selfie moment, but actually to intervene, albeit gently and to offer people what they need before they know how to name it?
Jay:	You mean like… emotional hospitality?
Sage:	Exactly. Like the bellboy in Tokyo who gave me tea when I felt lost. That cup did more for me than any spa menu.

Hervé:	It's a real paradox, you know. That kind of miswanting runs the market. People seem to think more equals better. But actually, I think that better often begins with less, less noise, less pressure, less pretence.
Jonas:	Right and fewer layers or barriers between people. That's why we're working with my team at the moment to drop that kind of 'performance'. We want to be polished, yes. But we really need to be real. And honestly, guests notice.
Jay:	But we're in business, right? So how do you sell that sense of… what is the right word… presence?
Hervé:	Well I think it's definitely not with slogans. But I really think we can make huge changes with design. With culture. All that stuff. But we also need to have the courage to lead instead of pander.
Sage:	That's all true for sure and I'd just add restraint to that list. I really think luxury isn't about more any more. It's about enough, done beautifully and with care.
Jonas:	Sometimes I walk through our new suites and wonder if the real amenity is the absence of distraction. No screens, just light, quiet and a view. And someone who listens to what you need.
Jay:	*(Sincerely)* I'd book that.

Conclusion: From Illusion to Impact

We hoteliers have always been in the business of dreams. We know how to impress. We know how to deliver. We build suites that shine, spas that soothe and restaurants that dazzle. But in the quiet moments, in the soft dissatisfaction behind a guest's smile, we also know something else, they're still not fulfilled. It's not because the room is wrong. It's not because the service is a failure. It's because the wanting itself is misplaced.

The more we understand this, the more clearly we see that our role is no longer to simply respond to what guests ask for. Our calling is greater: to gently guide them back to what truly nourishes them. This is not a rejection of luxury. It is its elevation. So perhaps now is the time to reframe our approach. What follows are gentle shifts in perspective we suggest we all should consider embracing.

1. From Fulfilling Desires to Deeper Needs

Guests arrive with curated wish lists, dreams shaped by marketing and comparison. They show us what they think they want.

As hoteliers, perhaps our role is not just to fulfil, but to notice what's beneath the request. To offer what's quietly missing.

2. From Material Opulence to Emotional Fulfilment

Marble glows. The lighting is perfect. The amenities are world-class.

And yet, still, a guest may feel untouched.

Let us consider how design can speak to the heart as well as the eye. How moments, not things, are what truly linger.

3. From Amplifying Expectations to Calibrating Them

Social media has rewritten what guests expect before they even arrive.

There is beauty in offering honest previews. In showing the magic and the mess. In designing an experience that surprises by being real.

4. From Performance to Presence

Infinity pools are photographed but not touched. Meals are styled, but not savoured.

Perhaps the real luxury is the time and space to be present. To forget the lens. To be there, in the moment, uninterrupted.

5. From Independence to Togetherness

Wealth buys privacy. But privacy can become isolation.

Even in our most exquisite suites, guests can feel completely alone.

What if our hotels quietly encouraged connection? Through design. Through ritual. Through the gentle warmth of a shared moment.

6. From Overbuilding to Understatement

We've all seen it: spas no one uses, restaurants that dazzle in photos but sit half-empty.

It may be time to build less, but more meaningfully. To trust that enough, done beautifully, is more than sufficient.

7. From Noise to Stillness

In a world that celebrates speed and spectacle, stillness has become rare.

Let's consider: can silence be an amenity? Can a moment of pause be the most generous gift we offer?

8. From Product-Centric to People-Centric

Guests return not for hardware, but for heart. For the person who noticed. The one who remembered.

There is always room to invest more in the people who are the experience. It's relationships, not renovations, that build loyalty.

9. From Trend-Following to Cultural Leadership

Guests often ask for what the world tells them to want.

And yet, some of the most powerful moments come when we offer what they didn't know to ask for. Quiet leadership. Courageous hospitality.

10. From Luxury as Display to Luxury as Sanctuary

Luxury has long been something to show. But more and more, guests seek something they can feel, something safe, human and honest.

What if our hotels became sanctuaries from performance? Places where people could let go and just be?

None of these shifts are mandates. They are possibilities. Invitations. A compass pointing toward a hospitality that heals rather than hurries, one that uplifts rather than overwhelms.

As hoteliers, we already hold space for beauty. Perhaps now, it's time to hold space for meaning, too.

CHAPTER FIVE
Needs

In a world that moves at breakneck speed, where trends flicker and fade faster than ever, there remains a single constant: human need. The way we travel has changed. The technologies we use, the expectations we hold, even the languages of luxury have evolved. But beneath it all, what people truly need, emotionally, psychologically, spiritually, has not changed. Not in centuries. Not ever.

This chapter is an invitation to return to that foundation.

For hoteliers, the ability to understand and serve human needs is not just a skill, it is a competitive advantage. And yet, all too often, the industry's energy may be misdirected toward surface innovations, such as design statements and technological upgrades. These may delight for a moment, but they rarely endure.

What endures is relevance. And relevance begins with need.

In these pages, we travel from ancient history to modern neuroscience, from guest feedback to missed opportunities. We unpack not just what guests say, but what they need. We reveal the subtle clues that guests leave behind. We warn of missed opportunities when the industry overlooks these basics and the chapter closes with a vision of the ideal home, a place where hospitality restores a taste of unconditional care, helping guests feel safe, valued and at peace.

This chapter offers no formulas. No shortcuts. What it offers is a way of seeing, a discipline of observation and empathy that reshapes how we think about design, service and strategy. It is, at its core, a return to first principles:

Who are our guests? What do they need?

And how do we honour those needs, every time, everywhere and for everyone?

If we can answer those questions with sincerity and skill, we do more than satisfy a customer. We restore something sacred: the feeling of being understood.

It is a call to see hospitality not as spectacle, but as the art of honouring some of the most fundamental aspects of being human.

Part One
Human Needs as the Foundation

The Constants Beneath Change

Needs don't change over time. This may seem like a bold statement, but take a moment to reflect and look around you. What you'll see is that despite the vast changes wrought by the pace and complexity of our modern world, fundamentally, the core needs of human beings remain unchanged. The need for love and recognition, for physical comfort and safety, the urge to communicate, to grow, to belong; these have persisted through the centuries. However, what does change is the way we meet these needs.

As hoteliers navigating a sector in constant flux, we can perhaps hold onto a reassuring truth: our guiding light does not move. Human needs are the lighthouse, they anchor us, orient us, bring clarity amidst the fog of evolving trends. Ultimately, if we focus on satisfying needs, we will always be relevant.

Our task, then, is not to chase change blindly, but to ask timeless questions in timely ways: Who are our guests? What are their needs? How can we best satisfy those needs, now?

This chapter returns to those questions repeatedly, because they are foundational to what we do. Everything begins there.

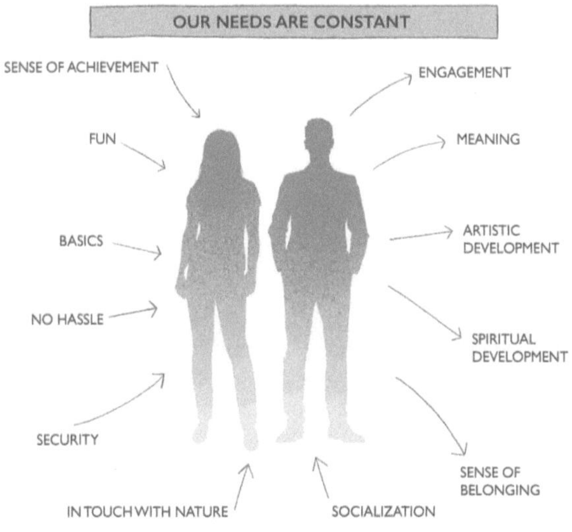

Communication: The Need That Waits for No One

We have always chased the horizon of immediacy, restless, impatient, reaching for news before it even arrives. The need to know, quickly and certainly, pulses through our history like a drumbeat. This need has driven innovations from carrier pigeons to social media, revealing that while technologies evolve, our needs remain unchanged.

But long before silicon chips and satellites, we taught the skies to carry our messages. The Persians likely began it, taming pigeons to deliver news on the wing. The Romans refined it, Caesar, it's said, dispatched birds as he conquered Gaul. The Greeks let their pigeons fly the names of Olympic champions to distant cities, their feathers bearing triumph across the sky.

Centuries passed, but the urgency remained. In the vast, rugged stretches of 19th-century America, the Pony Express galloped across the plains, relay riders in a dance with distance. For 18 months, it was the quickest line between Missouri and California. Ten days. That was the promise. Then came the telegraph and a new kind of communication; instant, electric, wordless wires pulsing across a continent, altering forever what it meant to be connected. Suddenly, ordinary citizens, farmers, workers, families and friends could send messages across the country in moments, reshaping not only how people communicated but how they imagined their place in a vast and newly intimate nation.

After this seismic shift, the tempo only quickened, telephone, telex, fax. Satellites blinked into orbit. Emails pinged. Mobile phones rang. Social media exploded across networks of 4G and 5G, turning the world into a single, ceaseless conversation.

Three thousand years of ingenuity, all devoted to fulfilling one persistent human yearning: Tell me now. The technologies have shifted, from runners on foot to printing presses, from telegraphs to TikTok, but beneath them all lies the same impulse. The methods change. The need does not. Our hunger for speed is not only about accessing information faster; it is about narrowing the gap between ourselves and others, about the hope that with enough signal, enough immediacy, we might finally bridge the distance that separates us. It is communication as closeness, a profound reassurance that we are not alone.

But speed isn't the only need that has endured. While some human longings race forward, others reach inward, into stillness, beauty and meaning. We do not only want to be heard now, we want to leave behind something that endures, to be heard anew in the future.

Artistic Expression: The Echo of the Soul

The need to express ourselves artistically is as old as humanity itself. On cave walls in Lascaux and Chauvet, early humans painted with earthy pigments not for survival, but to be seen, not only by each other, but by the divine, or by time itself.

As civilizations rose, so did temples, mosaics, sculptures and song. Art became a bridge between the earthly and the spiritual, a mirror of society and a rebellion against it. In every age, humans have reached for brush, chisel, or pen, to say: This is what it feels like to be alive.

Today, we construct culture digitally, sharing songs made on laptops, illustrations from tablets and poems written late at night in smart-phones' dull glow. The platforms change. The longing does not. Artistic expression is not decoration; it is declaration. It satisfies the soul's insistence that we be more than flesh and function. That we are seen. That we leave a mark.

Expression is one way the soul speaks, yet just as vital is its hunger to understand. To grow. To reach toward something greater within ourselves. Just as we've always needed to declare what we feel, we've also been driven to ask why things are the way they are.

Education & Self-improvement: The Climb Within

To grow is human. From the first questions of childhood, "Why is the sky blue?" "Where do people go when they die?", we are propelled by curiosity. In ancient times, knowledge was passed orally, through stories and parables. Later, scrolls and scriptures codified wisdom, but only a few could read them. Education was usually a privilege.

Over time, this changed. Monastic scribes gave way to schools. Printing presses unchained ideas. Universities became temples of thought, that gradually more and more could gain admittance to. And still the hunger grew, not just for facts, but for understanding. To learn is to expand one's inner world, to become a little less trapped in the present, a little freer.

In the digital age, knowledge is everywhere. We learn languages through apps, solve equations with videos, explore philosophy via podcasts. Yet the essence remains the same: growth. Self-improvement is not a luxury of the ambitious. It is a need embedded in our nature. We learn because we are incomplete. And in learning, we become.

Needs as a Mantra

We could illustrate each human need with countless examples, but the truth remains simple. Our fundamental needs remain largely unchanged by time or place. For us that means that every decision in hospitality can be tested against a single mantra: In what way does this action satisfy a guest's need? If the answer is unclear, or not anchored in a specific need, then the action may not be necessary at all.

But while these core needs may remain unchanged, the world around us does not. Societies move through sweeping, long-term transformations: demographic shifts, rapid urbanization, globalisation, rising complexity, higher education levels and improved living standards. These macro forces evolve over decades, shaping the terrain on which needs are expressed.

What makes this era feel like walking through quicksand is not just the change itself, but the speed of it. Technology acts as an accelerant. Trends now emerge, scale and shift almost overnight, crossing continents before we've had time to adapt. It's no surprise that this velocity can feel destabilizing.

Yet in the eye of this storm, the core truth remains: human needs do not change. When we return to them, clarify them, honour them, we can find our footing again.

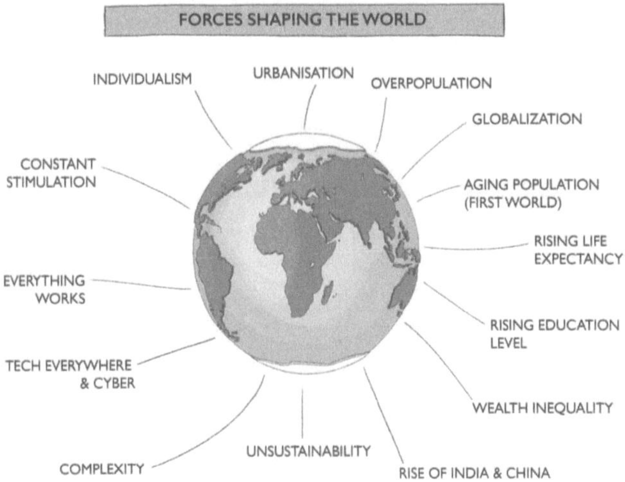

Part Two
The Guest's Voice

If change is the constant, then listening anchors to what's truly important. In fact, to understand how needs play out in a rapidly shifting world, we must hear directly from those we serve. Let us take you back to the pandemic, a moment in which many of us in hospitality found ourselves with a rare and unexpected commodity, time. With hotels temporarily quiet, lobby conversations paused and revenue meetings on hold, it became easier to connect with hoteliers across the globe. For once, there was room to reflect.

We all carry a mental to-do list of questions and projects we mean to get to when time allows, but that list always seems to grow, while those projects remain untouched. Near the top of ours were two long-held curiosities:

Can we define what "luxury" truly means in hospitality?

And, what makes a hotel experience great in the eyes of the guest?

We thought it would be a relatively straightforward process, a few conversations, some expert insight and a neat conclusion. But it didn't unfold that way. A handful of us met several times to discuss it, hoping to reach clarity. We read everything we could find, books, white papers, industry analyses. None of it gave us what we needed. Eventually, we agreed on a more grounded approach: ask the guests themselves.

With the help of participating hoteliers, we gathered roughly 1,800 guest comments. These came primarily from anonymised guest letters and online survey results, generously shared by some of the world's most respected properties. We supplemented and cross-referenced the data with publicly available online reviews. In total, the dataset included feedback from approximately 25 hotels, all of which regularly feature on the Condé Nast Traveler, Travel + Leisure and other top travel lists. From this raw material, we began a methodical process.

First, we sorted the comments into emerging themes. Then we undertook a semantic analysis, the careful work of drawing meaning from language. Guest feedback, in its natural form, can be rich but disorganised. It needs translation. With each round of analysis, the picture became clearer. Slowly, we moved closer to defining what luxury really meant to those who experienced it. There were four key findings and the results surprised us.

Finding 1: Hardware vs. Software

Let's begin with the obvious. The hotels we surveyed spared no expense when it came to design. They enlisted the world's most sought-after names including Philippe Starck, Thierry Despont, India Mahdavi, Pierre-Yves Rochon, David Collins and others. They even sourced the finest materials such as Carrara marble, Baccarat crystal, Pierre Frey fabrics, Frette linens. In many cases, millions were spent per room.

So, how did this impact the guests? Incredibly, of the 1,800 comments, only 2.6% mentioned design or materials at all. And even more strikingly, 75% of those rare comments about the 'hardware' were negative. Despite the staggering investment in design, despite the prominence of the names behind it, the guest response was nearly silent and when it wasn't, it often reflected dissatisfaction. The reality is simple, guests expect their physical environment to function and to be beautiful. That is, it's no longer a differentiator, it's a given. It becomes noteworthy only when something goes wrong.

Although a handful of guests, particularly those booking for special occasions, may still be wowed by opulent materials, the core demographic for luxury hotels, high-net-worth individuals (HNWIs), are not impressed. This is because, as we noted in chapter four, their homes often surpass even the grandest hotel suites in both design and material quality. The result is that the very investments designed to signal "luxury" are, for the most part, invisible to the people they are intended to impress. But perhaps luckily, guests on the whole are not interested in being impressed. They are looking for something else entirely.

WHAT IT TAKES TO BE LUXURY IN HOSPITALITY - MATERIAL ASPECT

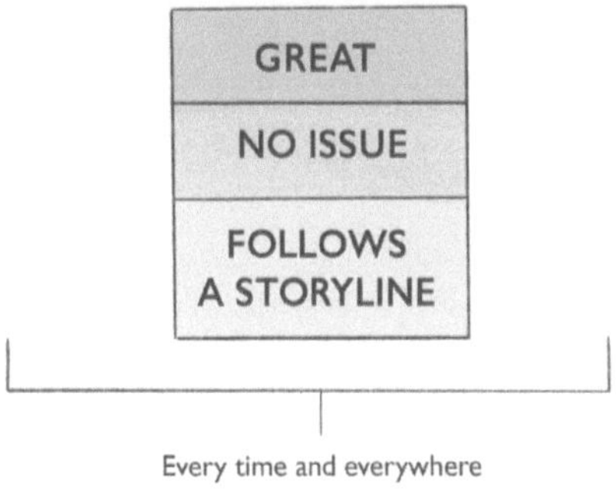

Finding 2: Service and People

When it comes to what truly defines guest satisfaction in a luxury hotel, one answer consistently rises to the top: service and people. While we, hoteliers, understand this instinctively, there's something powerful about seeing it confirmed again and again in the empirical data. Guest comments say it plainly:

> *"Our room was beautifully appointed and included all the extras one would expect. The location is perfect. There are numerous Michelin-ranked restaurant choices within the hotel. However, what makes this so unique (particularly when professionalism appears to be a lost art at too many hotel locations) is the high level of trained and friendly service one receives throughout the entire building."*

> *"The performance at your hotel is driven by service, service, service. The owners and managers of this hotel have succeeded at instilling a joyful sense of customer service that I wish I found in many more places."*

What's also notable is that when the level of service is not where it should be, even the most beautiful hardware and design won't make up for it:

> *"In terms of its palace peers in Paris, its hardware (being newer) is superior to every competitor. Unfortunately, the beauty and quality of the environment was let down by the service attitude and attention to detail."*

These comments speak volumes. They show that for all the investment poured into architecture, design and amenities, the lasting impression is created by people.

And more than that, that guests know exactly what they're looking for when it comes to service. Their language is precise and well defined. Their feedback falls into three distinct categories, each built around a precise set of words and carrying its own meaning: attitude, the spirit in which service is given; interaction, the way service is delivered; and mindset, the deeper professional values that guide behaviour.

Perhaps unsurprisingly guests rarely use jargon. They don't talk about KPIs or service models. But they express clearly what matters to them. It's not complicated. But it is significant. And when hotels get the people part right, guests return. They remember names. They write letters. They share stories. They advocate. They feel at home.

Attitude

Our guests defined a winning Attitude by three groups of words. At first, we were surprised by the simplicity of the responses. But when we analysed the data further, it became clear that although the words themselves were commonplace, they carried surprising depth of meaning: friendly, kind and warm; genuine, sincere and authentic; enthusiastic, happy and full of spark.

Guests who have everything in life, who have travelled the world over and stayed in the grandest hotels on the planet, appreciate above all people who are friendly, genuine and warm.

The Power of Warmth

Busy airports and over-crowded streets in cities can be harsh, unkind places. Everyone is fending for themselves in a society which is becoming ever more individualistic. Everyone is looking for the next safe haven. So hotel guests know when they have crossed the threshold into a real oasis of friendliness.

They feel physically good as soon as they recognise warmth, kindness, care, clearly expressed in the smile and body language of a welcoming member of hotel staff. When such signals are consistent over a couple of days most guests feel like they can finally relax.

As warmth, kindness and care are usually emotions reserved for either friends or family, they set the tone for a relationship and open the door to building relationships further.

> *"Wonderful hotels, including yours, excel at providing fine service, guest room comfort, well-considered amenities and even fun treats. But to us, what sets your hotel apart from the rest is the pervasive atmosphere of genuine warmth created by the staff. In the professional world, it is rare to find this, yet absolutely unmistakable when you're wrapped in it."*

The Weight of Authenticity

Why is genuine such a potent word? Because most interactions in the modern world are transactional. Guests, especially those who travel frequently or hold high positions, are constantly served, but rarely feel seen. What they long for is an experience that transcends the script. A moment that feels personal, human, unscripted.

In our earliest relationships, those with parents, caregivers and childhood friends, love and care were hopefully given unconditionally.

These original relationships shape what we continue to seek as adults; forms of authentic connection that are not dependent on money, status, or obligation. These forms of authentic connection have the power to powerfully impact the people we care for. Consider the guests who left London for Rome, only to receive a gift and handwritten note, sent by the receptionist they had met days earlier.

> *"We were so wonderfully surprised and pleased to receive a gift from you, personally delivered to the St. Regis in Rome with a beautiful note on your hotel stationery. You clearly picked up in our conversation upon checkout that we were heading to Rome. One of our great memories of that city is that you, on your own time, thought of us and went out of your way to send those personalised luggage tags. Amazing!"*

When employees do something that is above and beyond their job description, it becomes an act of genuine kindness and for this couple, this genuine act of kindness might have meant more than seeing the Coliseum.

The Joy of Spark

Why is that spark, that joyful enthusiasm that guests identified, so powerful? To reach the highest levels of guest experience, a good mood and genuine cheerfulness are essential, especially when situations are challenging. Clients love sensing that staff members are happy to provide service and that the team works together with ease and enjoyment.

Most people, including hotel guests, are naturally polite and do not like to feel they are imposing. They often hesitate to ask for services because they understand it may create extra work for team members. As a result, guests may not fully benefit from the expertise of professionals like concierges or receptionists.

But when staff make it clear that service isn't a burden but a source of pride and pleasure, it transforms the guest experience. Guests can take full advantage of what's offered, feeling truly special, without the discomfort of feeling awkward or guilty.

Below is a long but telling comment from a well-travelled professional. The final sentence of her reflection could serve as an inspiring aim for any hotel team.

> *"I travel constantly for business and occasionally for pleasure. I've stayed in top hotels around the world and I've never had an experience quite like the one at The Beaumont. John at the concierge desk went above and beyond, handling complex requests not only efficiently, but joyfully. Catarina and her staff were equally attentive and generous. We were there under stress, preparing for a high-stakes interview with the Prime Minister just hours after a terror attack. We probably weren't easy guests. Yet we were treated as though each of us were the most important person staying at the hotel. Though I've stayed at places offering VIP treatment, what moved me here was that we were 'ordinary' guests, yet received extraordinary care. I've never written to a hotel after a stay. But this time, I had to. Thank you for making a working trip feel like pleasure."*

Interaction

If *attitude* is about heart, *interaction* is about will.

Throughout our research we found that in the very best guest interactions, staff weren't simply friendly, they were helpful, in ways that ranged from thoughtful to extraordinary. Guests responded with deep appreciation when team members went beyond the call of duty; they were even more delighted when staff broke the rules on their behalf; and they felt genuinely cared for when it seemed that nothing was too much to ask.

Comments like "they really made an effort" appeared often and staff who were described as "attentive" or "unobtrusive" were held in particularly high regard. The best interactions were marked not by scripts, but by a kind of intuitive generosity, service that transcended the job description and entered the realm of the personal.

Acts that go beyond the expected, whether large or small, signal something powerful to guests: *this is not a transaction. This is a relationship*. And in that moment, the guest relaxes. The defences fall. They are in safe hands.

In the course of our research, we identified five types of behaviour that consistently earned guest praise for going "beyond the call of duty":

1. Doing what isn't in the job description

When staff step outside their defined roles to delight guests, the experience is unforgettable. These moments may feel serendipitous, but they are born of genuine attentiveness to what a guest needs.

> *"Each room has a butler, but these are not your average butlers. Mine even painted my fingernails for me when I was running late. That moment turned my day from stressed to blessed."*

What might have seemed small was, in fact, significant. That guest felt understood, pampered and seen.

2. Running errands well beyond the hotel's domain

Guests are continually surprised when the hotel's care for them extends beyond its four walls.

> *"I needed them to go to a comic bookstore and pick up books for me. They did so without hesitation and the books were waiting for me when I arrived at 8 a.m. No charge, no fuss, just kindness."*

The errand itself was ordinary. The generosity behind it was not.

3. Bending the rules for the guest's benefit

At the best hotels, systems serve people, not the other way around. When staff choose flexibility over rigidity, it's not a failure of process, it's a triumph of guest-centric thinking.

> *"They even arranged for us to have breakfast the day we left, earlier than they normally open. No one said, 'We can't.' They just made it happen."*

This is service elevated, not by rigid policy, but by teams trusted to use judgement and care.

4. Taking responsibility for problems that aren't theirs

Perhaps the most generous act is to step into a problem that is clearly not the hotel's fault, yet choose to solve it anyway.

> *"My son left for the airport without his passport. I was travelling alone with my children and completely overwhelmed. Within minutes, the front desk had it in a taxi and coordinated its safe return to him at Heathrow. Thanks to their calm, their speed and their professionalism he made his flight. I will never forget it."*

These moments move beyond the realm of service. They become important memories.

5. Persisting where others would give up

Perseverance is a rare form of dedication that guests never forget, especially when it's unexpected.

> *"The concierge suggested a sold-out play. Every day, they checked again.*

> *On the final day, there was a cancellation and they got us tickets. They didn't have to. But they did. And that spirit is why we'll return."*

Persistence communicates not only commitment, but a quiet kind of loyalty to the guest's happiness.

When we look closely at these stories, a pattern emerges. It's not about extravagance. It's about intent. True hospitality shines through interactions where staff demonstrate:

A willingness to go further.

A sense of ownership over the guest's experience.

And a desire to serve that feels effortless, human and kind.

Mindset

Throughout our research we discovered that when it comes to professional values, guests consistently ranked "attention to detail," "attentiveness," "anticipation," and "personalisation" as the most important. What makes attention to detail so powerful is that it conveys care. A small, thoughtful gesture carries an intimacy that goes beyond service, it feels personal. This is because we usually experience this kind of care from those closest to us, those who know us deeply and are willing to make an extra effort. Like a considerate partner or friend who surprises you with something meaningful, whether it's a planned celebration or in a moment of spontaneous affection.

To be on the receiving end of consistent, thoughtful attention is to feel as though you're in a deeply fulfilling relationship.

As Daniel Kahneman notes, a series of small, positive moments tends to leave a more lasting impression than even a single grand gesture. The emotional impact of being so deeply considered is difficult to quantify; it's rare, uplifting and at times profoundly moving.

> *"It's a fantastic hotel with fantastic service... The madeleines have gold leaf on them. As goes the phrase, 'If I can't trust you with the little things, how can I trust you with the big things?' It's amazing touches like that which make staying here a bucket list kind of experience."*

The Hidden Power of Anticipation

When this sense of attentiveness and care extends forward in time, when it's woven into the kinds of preparation we do for guests in advance, then it deepens into anticipation. In fact, when guests can sense that the team has been preparing for their arrival with the intent of enhancing their experience, the impact is significant. Even the smallest gestures stand out when they feel relevant and intentional.

Anticipation is made possible by effective systems, clear communication and a shared commitment from every team member. It requires that the employee not only knows who the guest is, but also actively seeks out details that allow them to anticipate the guest's needs, even down to a warm, personalised welcome. Delivering this level of experience involves careful observation, strong coordination and the initiative of someone empowered to act.

> *"What do you say when you ask your hotel for iron and board and they answer that they already took the liberty of pressing the pants you'd hung in your dressing room to wear to the big event tomorrow?*

When those anticipatory details are missed, guests are often forgiving, but not indifferent. Even subtle gaps can be noticed. While these lapses may be mentally filed away as "minor," their emotional resonance can linger.

> *"My only let down is that when we checked in, we weren't welcomed back and the young lady was lovely and started to explain the hotel. We have stayed here around 8 times and this is our 3rd stay this year. Surely it would come up on the computer as a returning guest, it's only minor but it is nice to be acknowledged as a regular guest. We saw another receptionist [the] next day and she immediately welcomed us and was pleased to see us. We always get a small gift and a personal note in our room. We had just flown from Australia. It's the small things that count. We are coming back next September for about 5 nights again and wouldn't stay anywhere else in London but fix the welcome back please!"*

Generosity as a Cornerstone of Luxury Hospitality

Generosity has always held a distinctive place in the guest experience. What guests cherish most is the feeling of being indulged, through thoughtful gestures, unexpected treats and complimentary touches. Again and again what emerges in guest feedback is that while people are willing to pay premium prices, they resent being "nickel and dimed."

In essence, guests don't want to be charged small fees for minor conveniences. Nor do they want to feel that hospitality is merely a function of the money exchanged. When everything carries a price tag, the opportunity to create a sense of genuine, unconditional care is lost. Each additional charge reinforces a purely transactional relationship, shattering the deep sense of ease and warmth that true hospitality aspires to create.

In contrast, at those rare hotels where extra charges fade into the background and generosity is freely expressed, guests take notice and they remember:

> *"We loved our room and its gorgeous bathroom with a large soaking tub and the complimentary minibar and snacks that were generously and daily refilled was a lovely touch. A coffee on the house is also delivered with every wake up call, a small thing but indicative of how the hotel feels like a home from home and there is no 'nickel and diming'."*

> *"Meant to tell you this story from last week. x has been in town this week staying at Hotel Y and The Beaumont. He is an old friend of mine so we had a drink. When at Hotel Y he asked the concierge for a ticket for the David Hockney exhibition – was told it was sold out but if he became an annual member of Tate for cost of £70 he would get a ticket immediately. He really considered this but decided the better of it. When he checked in at The Beaumont the concierge said is there anything we can do for you? Again he mentioned any chance of getting a ticket for Hockney. The*

concierge replied, it's virtually impossible and sold out, but why don't you borrow our Tate membership card and it will get you in! And he did, quite overwhelmed by the generous thoughtful behaviour."

Every Time, Everywhere, by Everyone

Stories like these highlight the magic of generosity, but they also raise the bar. A single act of kindness delights, yet what truly distinguishes the finest hotels is when such gestures aren't occasional surprises, but part of a culture practiced by every team member, every day.

Although guests perceive a hotel as exceptional when team members embody the right Attitude and Mindset and deliver the type of Interaction described above, there is one important caveat. Excellence is only truly recognised when it meets three conditions: Every Time, Everywhere, By Everyone.

If one team member rises to the occasion and delivers outstanding service, that makes them a great employee. But when everyone across the property does the same, consistently and without exception, then and only then, is it a great hotel. In the eyes of guests, relentless consistency is the hallmark of true excellence.

When an individual shines, guests are momentarily drawn into an atmosphere of care and ease and if the next encounter matches that same standard, the sense of hospitality deepens. With each consistent interaction, the guest's experience is elevated. But consistency is delicate. Once guests are lifted into that emotional space of well-being and care, even a single misstep, one lapse in attitude, one flat interaction, one missed opportunity, can burst the bubble.

WHAT IT TAKES TO BE TOP LUXURY IN HOSPITALITY - SERVICE & PEOPLE

ATTITUDE	INTERACTION		MINDSET
Friendly	Helpful	Nothing is too much	Great sense of anticipation
Genuine	Go beyond	Very attentive	Incredibly generous
Warm	Break rules		Omnipresent
Welcoming	Make an effort	Amazing attention to detail	Discreet

Every time, everywhere, everyone

Finding 3: How People Feel

Up to this point, we've focused on guest feedback related to the hotel's hardware, such as the building, design and furnishings and software, such as the service and the people. We refer to this as the Input. But perhaps even more important, though harder for guests to articulate, is how the hotel experience made them feel. This is what we call the Output.

Roughly 15% of guest comments include an emotional response, explicit expressions of how they felt. In many ways, these emotional reactions define a key goal for hoteliers: "When this happens, then I feel this way…"

Among the most commonly described emotions is the feeling of being at home. Guests express this in various ways, such as feeling "part of a family," or "part of a community." The second most frequent emotional outcome is feeling special. This too is phrased differently by guests, who say they felt "like a King or Queen," or even "like a movie star or rock star."

The phrase "home away from home" is often used in hospitality, but its meaning has been diluted through overuse. Yet when a guest genuinely feels at home, there does not seem to be a higher degree of elevation nor a higher praise or more powerful way to convey satisfaction.

> *"As a frequent traveller it is truly special to find a hotel that makes you feel like their only guest. A hotel who remembers you the moment you step through the door, remembers what you like and dislike and how you like it."*

> *"Have you ever thought about the fact that checking in at 3pm and checking out at 11am means the day in a hotel is only like 20 hours? No, why would you? Cause staying in a hotel most likely is all about having a place overnight. Believe me, you'll think about it at The Greenwich and you'll wish for that missing 4 hours. As staying here is staying with friends and at home at the same time. I can't say anything better about a hotel."*

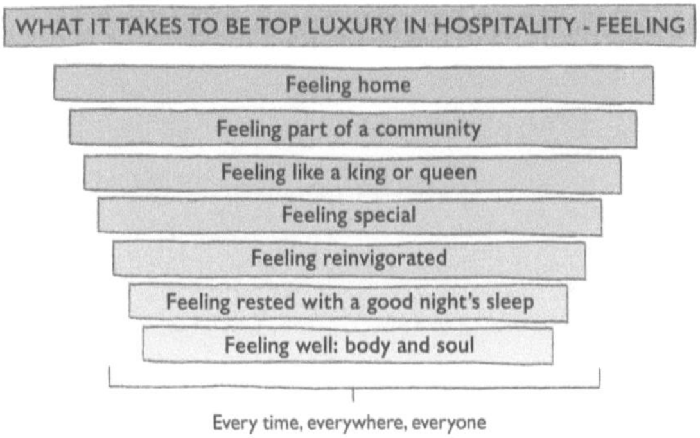

Finding 4: The Cherry on the Cake

Alongside the feeling of homeliness guests often describe hotels as truly exceptional when the property successfully solves a long-standing problem, something that frequently frustrates them in their travels or hotel stays. These are the kinds of issues that guests have learned to live with, often developing workarounds and accepting imperfection as the norm.

But persistent problems are exactly that, persistent. And when one hotel finally gets it right, guests don't just notice, they're elated. After years of irritation, finding a hotel that has thoughtfully resolved a nagging issue feels like discovering a little slice of heaven.

When reviewing feedback, it becomes clear, guests often write more passionately about small problems that are fixed than they do about million-dollar design features. At the Greenwich Hotel in New York, for example, the complimentary minibar generated more positive comments than its interiors designed by Axel Vervoordt. While the powerful shower got more mentions than its Italian restaurant run by a famous chef.

Elsewhere, when tipping was eliminated altogether, guests expressed overwhelming relief. Tipping might seem like a small thing, but its awkwardness is universal, yet rarely addressed.

Equally transformative was allowing guests to enjoy food or drinks anywhere in the hotel without having to sign a bill. That single change dramatically shifted the atmosphere and altered how guests felt during their stay:

> *"We didn't sign for anything the whole stay. Staff just knew us and our room number and never had to ask. That most likely is not the case with every guest and likely due to our length of stay but I have to tell you it was so nice to just get up and leave when we were done eating or at the bar. A great example of attention to detail of the guest and they almost all knew exactly what we were planning to order each night because they remembered."*

Many of these seemingly minor issues are still unsolved across the industry. Why, for example, is it so hard to get a decent cup of coffee in a luxury hotel? Guests have been conditioned to leave the building in search of a local coffee specialist for their caffeine fix.

As one guest said, fixing these "little" problems is what makes all the difference:

"There are three things that are just brilliant here and make me want to come back anytime! 1. I love your team! 2. I love your cappuccino (never had one like it before in a hotel) 3. You finally proved that you can have an intelligent light system in a hotel room and bathroom amenities that say what they are ... and you do not need glasses to read it!"

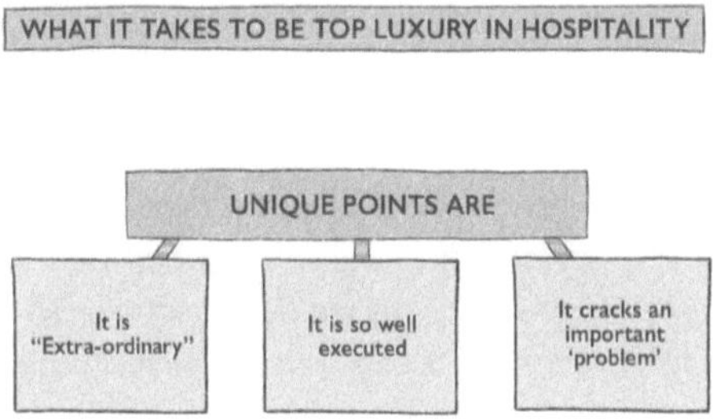

Part Three
A Deeper Perspectives on Needs

If solving long-standing frustrations creates delight, then understanding the deeper human needs behind those frustrations is what allows hospitality to move from problem-solving to truly transformative care. Fundamentally, no decision in luxury hospitality, be it the choice of bathroom amenities, the procurement of a hand-dryer, the design of porter protocols, or the approval of a new hotel blueprint, should be made without first answering our two fundamental questions.

Understanding who our guests truly are lies at the heart of every strategic move. The image we form of them profoundly influences not only the design of our spaces but also the delivery of our services. When the entire team shares a unified understanding of the guest, it transforms problem-solving into a collaborative endeavour.

Beyond marketing segments, psychographics, geography, purpose of trip, we must seek a deeper, more human definition. In our work, we were inspired by a charismatic hotel manager at The Lanesborough who offered a striking perspective: "A guest is a displaced individual." By this he meant that every traveller, no matter how seasoned, has stepped out of the comfort of their own home and thus on some quite deep level arrives in an unfamiliar place in a somewhat vulnerable state.

Taking a moment to sit with such a definition forces you to re-examine long-held assumptions and in doing so, it gradually changes the way you approach your work. As part of this process we began to engage with a wide range of different thought leaders, expanding our understanding and refining our idea of the guest. It is a journey we would encourage every hotelier to embark on, discovering for themselves what such a definition might mean in their own practice. Along the way, the insights of writers such as Johann Hari, Brené Brown and William Edwards Deming, enriched and sharpened our reflections, helping us see the guest through a broader, more human lens.

For example, in Lost Connections, Johann Hari set out to answer a simple yet profound question: "What causes anxiety and depression and what can solve it?" Through conversations with scientists from across the world, he identified nine causes of these afflictions, three biological or neurological and six rooted in disconnection:

1. Disconnection from meaningful work
2. Disconnection from others and community
3. Disconnection from meaningful values
4. Disconnection from status
5. Disconnection from nature
6. Disconnection from a secure and hopeful future

At first, we weren't sure what this meant for us, after all, Hari was writing about people struggling with depression. But as we reflected, we realised that these forms of disconnection touch all of us to some degree, including our guests. With that recognition, our definition deepened: a guest is not only *displaced*, but also disconnected. Now the question becomes: how do we care for someone in such a state?

Understanding Guest Needs

If guests arrive both displaced and disconnected, then understanding their hierarchy of needs becomes the first step in helping them feel whole again. Across the field of psychology, researchers such as Abraham Maslow, Frederick Herzberg and Clayton Alderfer broadly agree on three categories of human needs: basic, social and higher. Of these, social and higher needs, the needs related to the mind, spirit and soul, offer the greatest return when fulfilled.

And of these thinkers, it is perhaps Frederick Herzberg's motivation-hygiene theory that is essential reading for hoteliers. While we previously examined this in the context of staff motivation; here, it becomes a guiding principle in client satisfaction and investment strategy.

Guest surveys consistently reveal that the "hardware" of a hotel, its design and material finishes, functions as a hygiene factor.[7] Interestingly, in our surveys we saw that when this hardware is mentioned at all, it's typically in the context of failure. These aspects must meet expectations but rarely delight. In essence this means that investing in hardware brings a hotel only to the starting line.

But the real differentiators, the motivators, are rooted in human connection and the satisfaction of higher needs. These intrinsic factors warrant relentless attention and generous investment.

This distinction is well understood by forward-thinking brands like Soho House and 21c Museum Hotels. They invest just enough in quality hardware, always infused with style and channel the rest into programming that nurtures community, creativity and personal growth. At such properties, guests don't ask if something is happening, they ask what is happening and when.

A valuable metric in this context is the Key Performance Indicator: Important Needs Satisfied / Money Invested. This reframes success not in terms of vanity metrics or surface impressions, but rather, by linking investment directly to needs fulfilled, gives hoteliers a clear, practical lens through which to judge whether resources are being used wisely. It forces us to ask, for every pound, dollar, or euro spent, how much is a guest's well-being, whether physical, emotional, or spiritual, actually being improved. In this sense, it becomes not just a KPI, but a compass, stripping away subjectivity and helping leaders zero in on the initiatives, spaces and services that generate the deepest and most enduring returns.

The danger of ignoring this principle is evident in properties that feel like architectural masterpieces but leave visitors emotionally unmoved. A case in point: a famous Parisian hotel. In 2014, an €800 million investment for just over 200 rooms resulted in a space that, while opulent, was widely deemed soulless. Five exceptional general managers cycled through in less than a decade, each unable to reverse the consequences of a flawed foundational strategy.

Had the "Money Invested / Important Needs Satisfied" KPI been employed from the outset, early warning signs could have been identified. These leaders never stood a chance.

A much-anticipated opening in London's West End offers another cautionary tale. When it reopened in 2012 after a lavish redevelopment, The Telegraph's hotel expert, Fiona Duncan, described it as needing not just a redesign, but "something that money can't buy, soul." Despite impressive credentials, Sir David Chipperfield as architect and Piero Lissoni later appointed as interior designer of the refurbished lobby, the issue wasn't one of taste or talent. It was a strategic misstep: a design process detached from a clear understanding of guest needs.

In luxury hospitality, the brief must be sacred. It must emerge from a well-defined understanding of the guest's problems, because needs are, ultimately, problems to be solved.

But knowing what guests need is only part of the picture. We must also understand what stands in the way. What are the hidden problems they carry with them into our hotels?

The Problems Guests Carry

Today's guests, like many of us, navigate a world filled with complex emotional and societal challenges and they carry these struggles with them when they arrive at our doors. Anxiety is widespread, fuelled by technology, ecological crises, global instability and the relentless churn of information overload. Advertising, whether direct or woven invisibly through social media, constantly reminds us that we are "not good enough." Add to this the "always-on" syndrome, the psychological toll of perpetual connectivity and it is no surprise that more and more of us turn to substances and medications, from junk food to antidepressants, in search of relief.

The costs ripple further, as sleep deprivation has become a global norm, with the average night's rest shrinking by more than an hour in recent decades; eating disorders and food allergies are on the rise; and the erosion of connection, to nature, to community, to meaningful purpose, leaves many with a weakened sense of belonging. All these myriad burdens are carried by our guests, often silently, as they step into the world of hospitality.

While we can't possibly claim to solve all the challenges our guests face. These problems don't come from nowhere. They are symptoms of something deeper, a shift in how we grow up, how we're valued and what we learn to expect from the world. Here we turn to William Edwards Deming to help us understand this change.

From Unconditional to Transactional

William Edwards Deming, engineer, theorist and architect of Japan's post-war industrial renaissance, crafted a deceptively simple diagram that deserves the careful attention of every hotelier.

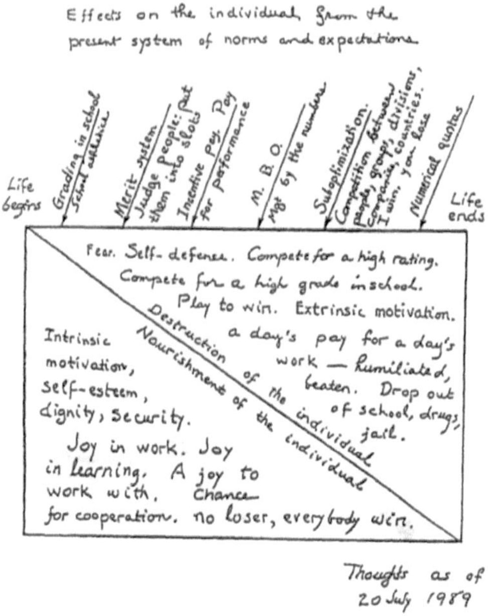

FIGURE 52
The Life Diagram
(Drawn by Dr. Deming)

His sketch charts the progression from childhood's unconditional love to adulthood's transactional world. Initially, we thrive on love freely given. Our relationships are loving and unconditional (at least in an ideal world). But over time, through school, sports, arts, we learn that praise and affection are contingent on achievement. Later, in professional and institutional settings, this conditionality intensifies. We are ranked, rated, rewarded and possibly even replaced.

Deming's key insight is that our intrinsic motivation, our natural desire to explore, learn, create, is slowly replaced by extrinsic incentives.

Imagine a young child in a sandbox who spots a football. He runs to it and kicks with all his might, not for reward, but for the pure, unfiltered joy of doing so. No one offered him five pounds as an incentive. He kicks because it feels wonderful to move, to express, to play. This is intrinsic motivation in its purest form.

As we age, systems often strip this away. We study for grades, not for learning; work for bonuses, not for growth; serve for tips, not for the joy of hospitality.

Deming's framework helps illuminate much of what we see and sense, from our guests. It suggests that at some point, we all fall from a kind of paradise. That state of unconditional love and unbridled joy or intrinsic motivation fades. But our soul and our body remember.

And so, our role as luxury hoteliers becomes clearer: to restore, even briefly, a taste of that lost paradise.

The Ideal Home

There are rare moments when we step into a home and sense something profound, this is a place where unconditional love and intrinsic motivation quietly shape the atmosphere. These homes do more than comfort; they awaken something deep within us. They carry us back to the earliest, most cherished period of many of our lives, childhood, when we were often loved not for what we did, but simply for who we were.

Such places become what we call the Ideal Home. More than bricks and mortar, an Ideal Home offers sanctuary. It is run not by obligation, but by purpose, by a family, a team whose motivation is genuine, self-directed and rooted in care. Their intent isn't to impress, but to nourish.

In this Ideal Home, guests often reconnect, subtly and unexpectedly, with their own childhood memories. The feeling of being seen, safe and valued resurfaces. It is as though, for a brief time, they've found their way back to paradise. The Ideal Home doesn't just meet needs, it restores joy and it welcomes with a warmth that feels rare in today's world.

Guided by the philosophy of W. Edwards Deming, we've reimagined the definition of a guest, not *merely as a customer, but as a human being in quiet need:*

A guest is a displaced and disconnected individual, digitally addicted, struggling with complex emotional and societal issues, seeking an Ideal Home to reconnect with unconditional love and intrinsic motivation.

And this leads us to the essential question: *How do you care for someone like this?*

There is an illustrative piece from Henry Vollam Morton's book In the Steps of the Master, published in 1934, that remarkably captures much of Deming's philosophy, though not through theory or analysis, but through lived experience and a deeply felt sense of awe, longing and almost childlike wonder. It captures Deming's work so completely that we believe it could well be framed and hung in every Hotelier's office.

> *"There is a state of mind for which there is, so far as I know, no name. It is not happiness, which is an active appreciation of things, neither is it contentment, which is placid and might be termed the evening of happiness. The only words that I can think of are so worn-out, debased and generally ill-used that they will probably make you smile. One is 'Well-being' and the other is our friend 'Love'. Everyone can, I hope, remember a time in childhood when this state of mind lasted not seconds but for days and weeks on end. Sometimes, by an effort of the imagination one attempts to*

project oneself back into those shining moments of life when the mind, untarnished by sin and undaunted by Eternity, lived as the butterfly lives, searching for and finding, only sweetness everywhere.

In those days, the earth smelt more richly and the sun seemed brighter than it is today; the rain, the snow and the mist were enchantments and we were unconsciously a part of the visible beauties which surrounded us. Life is to most a gradual growing away from this enchantment. But amid the million trials and difficulties it is possible now and again to recapture fractional seconds of this earlier world; so momentary are they that one is left wondering whether they ever happened, or whether they may be a stray memory of some other existence.

Missed Moments, Missed Needs

If the Ideal Home reminds us of hospitality's highest calling, then the story of the hand dryer reminds us of its greatest risk: forgetting the real needs in front of us. Where one offers a vision of soul and sanctuary, the other warns how easily even capable leaders can overlook the simple, unmet frustrations of daily life. Together, they set the stage for a crucial question: in our own industry, are we attuned to the deeper needs of our guests, or are we merely perfecting solutions to the wrong problems?

Not far from Chicago, the world's leading manufacturer of commercial hand dryers operated with confidence. In 2005, as in years past, the company was thriving. Every performance indicator flashed green. Profits were robust, sales were climbing and they held the largest market share in the industry. Customer satisfaction surveys consistently ranked them at the top. They were, without question, the dominant player in their sector. For more than three decades, they had focused on perfecting their product. Their engineering and innovation teams had invested years improving the design of commercial hand dryers installed in public restrooms across the globe. So, when the company's board of directors gathered just before Christmas in 2005, the atmosphere was one of deserved confidence and contentment.

The directors, all in their sixties, paused for a comfort break before settling into what promised to be a long meeting. In the restroom, they washed their hands and, as they had done countless times before, used one of their own hand dryers, products they were not only proud of, but personally and professionally familiar with.

Now, consider a typical hand-drying experience in 2005, one familiar to anyone who used a public restroom in those years. There might be a short queue at the dryers. Users would wave their hands awkwardly, attempting to activate the machine without touching the button. Then came the extended ritual of rubbing hands beneath the warm airflow. A small puddle would gradually form on the floor beneath the dryer. Frustrated by still-damp hands, people would either shake them off, wipe them on their shirt, or reach for paper towels as a backup. All the while, the loud hum of the dryer echoed not just in the restroom but often in nearby spaces as well.

Here, a critical question arises: what needs were left unmet?

- Hands were not fully dried. The job was not done.
- Hygiene was compromised.
- Paper towels were still needed, making the solution neither ecological nor economical.
- The dryers were noisy.
- The process was slow and led to queues.
- The puddles on the floor posed safety risks.

It takes less than a minute to articulate this list, yet for over thirty years, these issues went unaddressed by the world leader in the sector. The irony? Their leadership, engineers and employees used the product every single day. They were intelligent, experienced and well-resourced. And still, they missed the opportunity.

The story ends, as many do, when titans become complacent. A disruptor, in this case Dyson, entered the market and changed everything. Practically overnight, the world leader for 30 years lost its relevance. So what did Dyson do differently? They designed a product that:

- Dries hands fully in 18 seconds.
- Improves hygiene.
- Eliminates puddles on the floor.
- Removes the need for paper and uses less energy.
- (Yes, it's still noisy, but far more effective.)

By doing this they built a product that satisfied the user's actual needs and they reaped the rewards, becoming market leaders in record time.

While World Dryer sought to maintain its position in the market, Dyson sought to satisfy the needs of the end users. World Dryer continued refining the product without, it seemed, re-examining the core of the problem. Dyson began with a clear brief: a full and honest list of user frustrations, a catalogue of unmet needs. From that starting point, they engineered their solution.

Dyson's genius lies not just in product design, but in strategic empathy. They consistently choose sectors where leaders fail to meet customer needs. Their brief to engineers is precise and bold: find real answers to real problems. And they do. Not only did they dominate the sector, but they did so while selling machines at more than double the price of their competitors.

Everyday Stories of Unmet Needs and Lost Opportunities

In hindsight, gaps in the market often appear blindingly obvious. And yet, recognising them in real time takes something more: an alertness to the unmet need, a willingness to question the familiar. The world of luxury hospitality is filled with stories that shine a light on these missed chances, opportunities hiding in plain sight. Yet all too often, they remain unrealised.

Take the invention of the rolling suitcase. In 1970, Bernard Sadow developed the world's first suitcase on wheels. He patented it two years later, in 1972. That's more than 5,000 years after the invention of the wheel. How is it possible that humanity invented the wheel millennia ago and yet no one thought to attach it to luggage until the 20th century?

Nassim Nicholas Taleb, Professor of Risk Engineering at NYU and author of The Black Swan, also reflects on this strange oversight. After years of hauling heavy suitcases through airports and train stations, he admitted being stunned by his own passive acceptance of the inconvenience. In Taleb's view, the rolling suitcase is a metaphor, a parable of how we often ignore the simplest, most elegant solutions because we're seduced by the complex, the grandiose, the difficult.

The late arrival of the wheeled suitcase serves as more than just an innovation case study. It's a cautionary tale, a quiet reminder of how much low-hanging fruit remains in the world of hospitality, waiting to be seen through a different lens. The lens of human need.

Guests have been arriving at hotels with rolling suitcases for decades. They've dragged them through airport terminals, train platforms, cobbled streets and long lobbies. By the time they reach the hotel's entrance, they've often covered several kilometres, bag in tow.

And then, what happens?

A hotel porter appears. Often without asking, the suitcase is whisked away, for the final fifteen meters.

What does the guest know at that moment? They know their bag will disappear through a side door. They suspect they'll have to wait upstairs in their room before it's delivered. Once in their room, they hesitate to use the facilities, because the knock could come at any moment. And of course, they'll need a tip, in the local currency, ready in hand.

Is that really worth the last fifteen meters?

This moment, seemingly small, is a daily ritual repeated in hotels around the world. And yet, it reveals a missed opportunity that's persisted for decades. Since 1972, the hospitality industry has had every chance to adapt to this evolution in luggage and travel behaviour. Yet many have not. Instead of rethinking the guest experience around the suitcase on wheels, hotels have clung to a ritual rooted in outdated assumptions.

What might have been possible had hoteliers started with a different approach, one rooted in observing real behaviour, identifying unmet needs and designing from the guest's perspective? Instead of holding onto a ritual that frustrates more than it delights, hotels could reimagine arrival as a moment of empowerment rather than interruption. Guests don't necessarily need their bag carried, they need clarity, ease and a sense of welcome. A simple redesign of the process, clear signage, intuitive self-service options, or the offer of help only when genuinely wanted, would transform this moment. By starting from the guest's lived reality rather than tradition, hoteliers can replace inconvenience with relief, awkwardness with autonomy and an old ritual with one that signals genuine care.

Remember innovation in hospitality doesn't always require reinvention. Sometimes, it simply demands attentiveness, a shift in mindset. When we begin not with tradition, but with the guest's lived experience, the possibilities unfold. And the opportunities are no longer hidden, they are right there, waiting to be claimed.

Red Alert

In 99.9% of hotel rooms around the world, a television stands as a fixture of modern comfort. And with it, almost without exception, a small red light glows silently through the night. Whether the hotel is one-star or five, boutique or branded, new or old, in Tokyo or Toronto, that unblinking red dot is ever-present. It is one of the few constants across countries, cultures and categories.

In fact, 44% of people over the age of 40 report difficulty sleeping when exposed to light at night and that sensitivity only increases with age. And yet, who makes up the core clientele of most luxury hotels? Statistically, guests in their forties and beyond. These are the very individuals most vulnerable to nocturnal light disruption, yet they are also the ones paying a premium for rest, comfort and deep restoration.

The irony could not be starker. As one executive at Four Seasons Hotels aptly put it, *"If we can't give people a good night's sleep in a hotel, then what are we for?"*

Despite this, with each new hotel opening and every grand renovation, the industry continues to create rooms that unintentionally undermine the very thing our guests come for, rest. Architectural firms are engaged, hardware is upgraded, technology is layered into every corner and yet, this most basic of needs is consistently compromised.

And the red light on the TV is just the beginning. Guests also contend with the blinking glow of the smoke detector, the constant illumination of the air-conditioning display and the soft green hue of the telephone keypad. Add to this the blue light of the bedside radio, the bright shine from the back of the television and its tangle of cables and the slivers of daylight or city glare that slip through imperfect blackout curtains. Even the corridor light seeping under the door becomes part of this quiet assault. All together, these small intrusions conspire to make rest harder than it should be.

Guests notice. They mention it. They adapt. Many have developed small rituals to cope, hanging trousers over the TV, draping towels across devices, unplugging electronics, or repositioning pillows to block out unwanted glow. While experienced travellers now arrive equipped with eye masks and earplugs. These are not indulgences of luxury; these are coping mechanisms. These are workarounds for what should never have been a problem to begin with.

So why do we consistently overlook something so fundamental? Why do some of the world's most talented designers fail to factor in light pollution in their room concepts? Why do experienced hotel managers and owners sign off on designs that actively prevent sleep?

The answer is disarmingly simple: we start with the solution, not the problem.

We focus on aesthetic appeal, compliance codes, feature-rich products and forget to ask: what is the job to be done? If that job is to provide restful, uninterrupted, high-quality sleep, then preventing light pollution becomes a non-negotiable. We would spot it in seconds. Much like the list of unmet needs in the hand dryer story, the answer would reveal itself almost instantly, *if we simply framed the question correctly.*

This is not about complex innovation or expensive solutions. It does not require vast investment or exceptional intelligence. It requires a shift in mindset. A return to fundamentals. At its core, hospitality should be guided by our three deliberate and consistent questions: Who are our guests? What are their needs? And how do we satisfy those needs?

When these questions form the foundation of every decision, design, policy, service and product, the guest experience is transformed.

Too often, hoteliers, as well as designers, developers and asset managers, begin with products, features and compliance checklists. We get lost in materials and aesthetics, hardware and other features. We forget to start with the guest's needs.

And the guest's needs in this case are simple: they want to sleep. Not just sleep, but sleep well. Deeply. Rejuvenatingly. Quietly.

When that isn't the priority, no number of pillows or high-thread-count linens can make up for the hum of an air conditioner or the soft blink of a power light. The outcome? A guest who came to rest and instead lies awake.

The challenge is clear: we must think differently, shift our perspective. Start not with the product, but with the problem. Not with the solution, but with the need. In doing so, we return to the essence of luxury hospitality, offering peace, presence and profound rest in a world that rarely pauses.

Interpret the Signs

If the design stage fails to anticipate these needs, the responsibility shifts to the daily practice, the lived reality of service, where guests leave behind subtle but telling clues about what truly matters to them.

In this ongoing effort to meet our guests' needs, perhaps we should turn the task into a game, a treasure hunt played by every member of the team. The treasures? Clues. Clues that our guests leave behind, intentionally or not. Because they are always telling us something. We simply need to look and listen.

Often, the first clues come in the form of offhand comments:

"My room was lit up like a Christmas tree."

"There were more lights in my room than in a disco."

These aren't jokes. They are expressions of frustration, offered with a layer of humour to soften the truth. They speak of discomfort, experienced not once, but repeatedly.

Still, they leave signs, quiet, practical clues. A scarf or towel is draped over the TV to block its red standby light. An extra cushion rests against the blinking bedside clock. Sometimes, the TV itself is discreetly unplugged.

Each gesture is a whisper: *"This light kept me awake."*
Each one, a plea: *"Please help me sleep better."*

A curious, attentive staff member might pause to consider: Why did the guest move this? What discomfort were they trying to solve? And what can I do to prevent this from happening again?

It could become a kind of thoughtful detective work, a playful, purposeful exercise in service design. These seemingly small adjustments are not random acts. They are deliberate responses to an environment that failed to anticipate basic needs. They are invitations to see things through the eyes of the guest.

Yet too often, the clues are dismissed. The cushion is returned to its decorative position. The scarf is neatly folded. The room is restored to its original state, sometimes with a sigh of frustration at the guest who dared to rearrange it.

But a true guest understanding begins with observation at the most granular level. Every object moved, every light covered, every item unplugged is telling us something. These are moments of design failure revealed, not through surveys, but through behaviour.

The path to extraordinary service isn't always paved with grand gestures. Often, it's built on subtle awareness. If we are paying attention, guests will always show us what matters most. All we have to do is follow the clues.

Out of Focus

The same blindness that causes us to overlook these signals can also lead us to miss other, equally obvious guest frustrations. For example, with our executive teams, we can spend countless hours debating which bathroom amenities to feature. We deliberate over scents, packaging and prestige brands, often with sincere care and attention to detail. Once the final selection is made, the products are delivered to our properties and carefully arranged in guest bathrooms by the housekeeping team.

Each shower cubicle is then outfitted with three elegant bottles: shower gel, shampoo and conditioner. So far, so good.

But what happens next?

The guest enters the bathroom, removes their glasses and steps into the shower. The water is already flowing. Moments later, they reach out for what they hope is shampoo, only to realise they're guessing. The brand name is bold and easy to spot, but the actual product description? Printed in fine, delicate text, completely unreadable without glasses. In the steam-filled space, they have no choice but to take a chance. And all too often, the wrong product ends up being massaged into their hair.

It may seem like a small detail, but it's not a rare one. And it continues to occur, day after day, guest after guest.

Why?

Because while we invested time and effort into selecting the perfect brand and fragrance, we failed to map the guest journey completely. We didn't pause to ask the two questions that would have brought this issue to light in moments: who are our clients and what are their needs?

In luxury hotels, the average guest is over the age of 40. Many wear glasses. And nearly all remove them before stepping into the shower. This isn't a rare behaviour, it's a standard one. Yet it's rarely accounted for in the design of the experience.

Since we're on the subject of bathrooms, let's consider the shower system itself.

In many modern hotels, the shower has become a statement of style, all sleek fittings, minimalist dials, multiple heads and high-tech controls. But in the pursuit of beauty, function is often lost. How many guests, running on a tight schedule before a breakfast meeting, step into the shower expecting a quick refresh, only to be caught off guard?

One twist of a dial and water rains unexpectedly from the ceiling-mounted head instead of the handheld wand. Or the other way around. With no instructions in sight, guests are left to guess. Some receive an icy wake-up call as they stand in the line of fire, struggling to understand an unfamiliar system.

Weary travellers develop their own tactics, testing knobs cautiously, shielding themselves with towels, or simply stepping aside until they can safely determine the flow. And in walk-in showers where the main head is mounted at the far end of the stall, there's often no escape at all.

So again, we return to the two questions: who are our clients and what are their needs?

These are not questions of aesthetics or branding. They are questions of human experience. Of empathy. Of understanding the small, functional moments that quietly shape a guest's stay. These are not matters of luxury design, they are matters of everyday use.

The problem isn't a lack of care, talent, or intelligence. It's a lack of focus on the right questions. We fixate on the visual, the product, the prestige, without seeing the space through the eyes of the person using it, the focus should not be on what looks impressive in a brochure, but with what feels effortless in the hands of the guest. And until we make that shift, even the most elegant bathrooms in the world will still leave guests frustrated, uncomfortable and unseen.

A true luxury experience therefore anticipates not just what the guest sees, but what they feel, the ease, the comfort, the clarity of every interaction. It's not about designing a showroom; it's about creating a space that understands and responds to human behaviour.

And when we consistently return to those two foundational questions, we move from assumption to awareness. From awareness to thoughtful action. And from action, ultimately, to deep satisfaction of our guests' needs.

In these last couple of sections, we've explored a series of small but telling examples, most of which are easily resolved once recognised. But there is a deeper lesson here, that the true solution must begin much earlier, at the design stage. In fact, it's at the very start of a project, during the first concept brief, during menu planning, during space layout discussions, where our most important question must be asked.

When we lead with these questions, everything that follows, from the amuse-bouche to the lighting, from the linen to the layout, can be aligned with clarity, empathy and purpose. And that, ultimately, is where excellence in hospitality begins.

The Ideal Home, Realised

If small oversights can so easily erode the guest experience, then the case study of The Beaumont shows us the opposite: how an unwavering focus on human needs can transform a hotel into something more than luxury, something we discussed early in this chapter, an Ideal Home.

The Beaumont Hotel in Mayfair is a five-star retreat set in a Grade II-listed 1920s Art-Deco building. It's a striking place, not least because of its unusual backstory: the hotel was imagined around the fictional character of Jimmy Beaumont, a New York hotelier who, disenchanted with prohibition-era America, returned to London to create a haven of ease and sophistication.

When it opened in 2014, The Beaumont did not have the architectural grandeur or vast budgets of London's established icons. Its leadership instead leaned on clever storytelling, impeccable taste and a focus on a gap in the emotional landscape of luxury. This lacuna was the Ideal Home, a concept that had not been fully realised in hospitality. The Beaumont set out to change that.

Alongside the guidance of visionary owner Jeremy King, Jannes and his management team at The Beaumont began an intentional, five year journey. Every detail was reconsidered. They eliminated almost anything that did not align with the vision of creating the most elevated and nurturing version of home. At the same time, they cultivated something even rarer, unconditional relationships within the team. As one guest later observed, the staff seemed to "instil joy" and not just in the service, but in the very place itself.

Every guest was greeted by name, no matter where they were in the hotel. There were no signatures, no interruptions to confirm room numbers or names. Tipping was quietly replaced with a transparent service charge. Everything in the room, from refreshments to thoughtful extras, was included. Small gestures of warmth and care were not occasional, but instead repeated with consistency and intention.

The result was extraordinary. The staff were deeply motivated, not by scripts or incentives, but by the genuine pleasure of service. They loved making guests happy and it showed. Guests felt it. They caught the spirit of the place. The atmosphere, built on trust, joy and gentle generosity, resonated deeply. For many, it stirred memories of a time when life felt safer, simpler and full of wonder.

Some even wrote to say their stay at The Beaumont had changed them. It had helped them remember what mattered most. It had returned them, emotionally, if not literally, to a forgotten sanctuary. A place of love. Of home.

Scenario: Making Guests Feel at Home

Setting:	A staff meeting room, everyone gathered around some organic snacks.
Characters:	
Hervé:	A CEO driven to make a hotel feel like home
Claire:	The general manager
Lena:	The reception manager, attentive to the last detail
Dina:	The head housekeeper, conscious of guest's needs
Omar:	The restaurant manager, patient, thoughtful and discreet

Hervé:	We've often talked about the hotel as an "ideal home." But what do we think that really means in our day-to-day choices?
Claire:	I guess for me, it's when guests let their guard down. When they feel like they don't have to perform or protect themselves. I think that's when you know you've got it right.
Lena:	I think Claire's right and honestly it starts at check-in. When a guest sees that we remember their name, their preferences, the room they like, they relax. You can see it in their posture.
Dina:	It's immediate. It's in the warmth they give to staff. The fact that someone thought of them. Like clothes already pressed, the right tea on the tray, the temperature exactly how they like it. You can see it really makes a difference.
Omar:	I think the crux of it is giving people the kind of attention that makes them feel cared for without being managed.
Hervé:	Completely, so what we're saying is it's not about opulence. It's about familiarity, thoughtfulness and flow.
Claire:	Exactly. I think it's that true luxury is not being made to ask.
Lena:	Right, one guest once said to me, "it feels like returning to a friend's house I love." Honestly, that really stuck with me, because that's the goal: it should feel like a welcome back, not a check-in.
Dina:	I completely agree with Lena and I think that means we need to avoid things that feel

transactional. Because basically, if every little thing is priced, it undermines that sense of welcome.

Hervé: And that ties into what we discussed earlier. Generosity isn't about the money, it's about intention. A handwritten note, a pressed shirt, a favourite snack, these are the details that say to the guest, "You belong here."

Claire: I hear that. That's why we call it the Ideal Home. Not just clean and pretty. But emotionally safe.

Hervé: So, I guess the real question here is, where are we not yet delivering that sense of home?

Lena: For me I think it's for late-night arrivals. They often get the most minimal interaction and the welcome is pretty rushed. That's not how a home greets you.

Dina: Agreed. And our long-stay guests. We assume they're settled, so we stop surprising them with the quality of the care.

Omar: I think solo travellers too. Especially women. Sometimes they feel more observed than welcomed. That's something we need to fix.

Hervé: These are all good examples, thanks team. I think the next steps are for us to treat them all as design challenges. Let's think of it this way, if a guest walked into their own ideal home at midnight, or after three weeks away, what would be waiting for them?

Claire: Probably a warm light, a familiar scent, snacks, for sure and maybe even a note that says, "welcome home." That's not hard to create.

Hervé:	Let's keep asking that question, not just "What will impress them?" but "What will comfort them?"
All:	Agreed.

Conclusion: The Compass That Never Moves

Throughout this chapter we've seen how easily the industry can overlook even the most obvious frustrations and we've also seen what is possible when our guests' needs are met with clarity and empathy, hotels that feel like homes, service that feels like care, moments that restore something precious and rare.

The lesson of this chapter is then deceptively simple. Hardware, aesthetics and brand prestige may draw attention, but they are not what endures. What truly endures is the feeling of being understood. The experience of being welcomed not as a customer, but as a human being who is displaced, disconnected and in need of sanctuary. And it is to honour that reality that we believe is at the very heart of true hospitality.

This means then that needs must always remain our North Star, our compass. They do not flicker with fashion or fade with the rising of the latest trend. They stand steady, pointing us back to what truly matters. To serve them is to stay relevant; to ignore them is to drift into irrelevance, no matter how polished the product or how grand the property.

But recognising needs is only half the task. The greater challenge and the greater opportunity, is to translate this clarity into design, operations and culture. To build hotels that are not only responsive to the present, but resilient to the future and the changes it has to offer us.

CHAPTER SIX

Surrounded, yet estranged

Scenario:	**The Fire and the Grain**
Setting:	Lounge area, late afternoon. The fire is low but warm. Mr. Leclerc, mid-fifties, well-travelled, is admiring a piece of woodwork near the fireplace, a low stool, hand-carved and weathered smooth by time.
Characters:	
Mr. Leclerc:	A thoughtful guest.
Amina:	General Manager, observant and sincere.
Hervé:	CEO of the hotel group, seated nearby with a cup of tea, listening more than speaking.

Amina:	*(Approaching with a small smile)* You have a good eye, this is one of my favourite pieces too. It was carved by a local woodworker, Elise. She only works with reclaimed oak. This one actually came from a 150-year-old wine press.
Mr. Leclerc:	*(Smiling)* It shows and I really like the craftsmanship, it's definitely not the kind of run-of-the-mill furniture you usually see in places like this. Work-wise, I've ended up staying in a hundred hotels and honestly, they're pretty forgettable. But this place, actually might be a bit of an exception to that rule, it's definitely got something about it, a different atmosphere…
Amina:	We've tried to build the hotel almost like a story, but one that's told through its materials, its history and the people who shaped it. It's been a lot of work, but that's why Elise and the other local artisans we work with are so important to what we do.
Mr. Leclerc:	Interesting, I actually walked by the bookbinding room this morning and had a bit of a peep. That's not common in a hotel and I'd be interested in checking it out some time.
Amina:	Yeah, I love that place. It's part of this whole living craft project. Basically, we didn't just want a space for demonstration, we wanted one where people could actually make things. Full presses, cutting tools, stitching frames, even traditional inks. We wanted it to be a working space from the get-go.

Mr. Leclerc: But isn't it a bit of a risk, to dedicate a whole space to something that doesn't directly generate revenue?

Hervé: *(Gently, from his seat)*
I suppose that isn't the only way we think about value, especially in the long-term. We're thinking about it also in terms of relationships and the significant memories people make here, things that they learn and take with them into the wider world.

Amina: Right, and the bookbinding room isn't just about books honestly. People slow down there, start conversations with each other, they might even repair an old notebook, or bind a few loose pages together. We hope they leave thinking differently about memory, permanence and the things they carry through their lives.

Mr. Leclerc: That's fascinating, I don't know many other luxury places, if any, that are trying to put more meaningful experiences at the core of what they offer.

Amina: Exactly. We're trying to return to more traditional ideas of what luxury used to mean, in terms of rarity, detail and that more human touch. Working in the sector, so many hotels are caught between service and spectacle and that can kind of end up with a guest experience that's not necessarily that restful. So, we're trying to offer something different built around stillness, so guests have a chance to just take a moment and reconnect with themselves.

Mr. Leclerc: So, in this way of thinking about things, you want the hotel to be more than a place where people stay, but an expression of the good life in some way?

Amina: *(Nodding)*
In an ideal world this is a place that reminds you it's possible to live differently, if it's just for a few days.

Mr. Leclerc: That reminds me of something I saw in a ryokan in Kyoto once. It was a ceiling made from 300-year-old cedar. The owner told me the craftsmen pruned the trees by hand for generations to avoid knots.

Amina: *(Smiling)*
Hiiragiya? Room 52?

Mr. Leclerc: *(Delighted)*
You know it?

Hervé: Yes, it's a place we both love. Mrs. Nishimura's ryokan was actually a key inspiration for the whole culture we've tried to develop here. You know, that kind of quiet luxury, with actual relationships and where all the objects really feel handmade. And even made by a person guests can actually meet.

Mr. Leclerc: Honestly, it's great. And I think it's working because I've had more meaningful conversations here in one day than I've had in a week elsewhere.

Introduction: A Crisis of Connection

We live in a world surrounded by objects we no longer understand. For many of us, the objects that fill our lives are made far away, in countries we rarely visit, by people we never meet and through processes we cannot explain. The factories, workshops and craftspeople who once existed in, or near, our communities have largely disappeared. This distance has left us anxious, dependent and strangely helpless, unable to repair what breaks, unsure which choices are sustainable and increasingly disconnected from the meaning of things.

Yet, the need for craft and human touch has not disappeared; it lingers in the fascination of watching a potter at work, in the growing popularity of cooking (both on TV and in real life) and in the awe we retain when seeing something made by hand. This chapter explores what we lose when making disappears, what we gain when we keep it alive and how hotels can become sanctuaries where guests reconnect with craft, story and the human side of the material world. We'll consider the psychological cost of disconnection, the urgency of preserving embodied knowledge, the resilience of cooking as our last widespread craft and the ways in which traditions, stories and thoughtful hospitality can help us weave meaning back into the material world.

The change we describe is more than economic, it is deeply psychological, cultural and emotional. A key part of it is that most of us no longer know how to make, fix, or even explain the materials and objects we use every day. When something breaks, we are rarely able to repair it; so instead, we throw it away and buy a replacement.

This shift creates four key problems:

- It creates anxiety, an unsettling sense of no longer understanding the world around us.
- It fosters dependence, as we find ourselves utterly reliant on distant factories and global supply chains.
- It breeds helplessness, since the people and skills that once made everyday life function are now out of reach.
- It sows distrust: how can we truly trust the products we use if we don't know who made them, or how, or sometimes even why?

These forms of disconnection are made even more painful when combined with a growing awareness about sustainability. Many people want to make ethical choices, but often find they can't. This is because it's often such a challenge to know which product is genuinely better for the planet, especially when greenwashing is everywhere. Not only that, but repairing can be harder than replacing, when a single broken plastic piece can send a whole kettle to the recycling bin. In the end, even the decision that seems right can still feel wrong.

At the core of this modern discomfort is a nagging, constant feeling:

> *"I am surrounded by things I cannot relate to, cannot trust and cannot fix."*

A Sense of Urgency: We Are the Last to Remember

This is also a generational concern. Today, there are many who still remember a different world. A world where you could fix your own car, where a Renault 4 could be mended with a few tools, plenty of elbow grease and a little know-how. Where, as a child, you could walk into a local workshop and ask for help from a qualified iron welder, carpenter, or tailor and even end up apprenticing there. But that world is fading fast.

The factories that migrated overseas during forty years of globalisation are unlikely to return as spaces for human labour. If they return at all, they will return as robot-run production sites. The rhythm of machines may soon replace the rhythm of skilled hands. And so, the question becomes even more pressing:

What happens to our culture, our bodies and our sense of meaning when our hands are no longer needed?

We can already see how visibly rare and emotionally powerful human craft has become. When we travel to countries less blighted by offshoring, there is often a fascination in encountering places where making is still visible. In the souks of Marrakesh, for instance, it's not the shops that usually captivate people most, it's the producers that are still on-site. You can wander through back alleys and see metalworkers, woodworkers, whitesmiths, all with tools in hand, making and mending in real time.

Watching a woodworker using their feet to hold their tools, carving a chess piece with nothing but the strength of their hand, is to watch a kind of grace in action. The air is filled not just with dust and scent, but with wonder; that deep, childlike awe of watching something emerge from raw material through pure human effort.

These moments stand out precisely because they've become rare. They reveal something we're missing and something we still crave. But this isn't just about preserving the past. It's about making sure we don't lose a core part of what it means to be human.

The Living Craft: How Cooking Still Connects Us

Amid this loss, one practice has not disappeared, in fact, it has flourished: cooking. Why are chefs and pastry chefs so popular today? Why are people obsessed with cooking shows, recipe books and kitchen tools? Because cooking is craft. It is tactile, sensory, creative and immediate. It connects us to raw ingredients. To producers and farmers. To our gardens, our land and our hands. When we cook, we transform something with care and intention. We directly taste the result of our labour, share it and take pride in it.

Cooking holds the essence of what we've lost elsewhere: a sense of locality, the embodiment of skill, the care of craftsmanship, the strength of community and the richness of a story that's told in every object.

Cooking shows us how one simple, everyday act can rebuild trust, rediscover joy and reinvent healthier ways of living from the grassroots up. It is a template for how we might approach making and mending across other parts of life; not as a burden, but as nourishing rituals of connection.

A Historical Echo: The Mingei Movement and the Fight for Craft

This is not the first time in history that people have felt the need to protect traditional forms of craft from the tide of industrialization. In early 20th-century Japan, a small group of visionaries recognised the danger posed by mass production to the cultural and spiritual value of handmade things.

Led by philosopher and aesthete Soetsu Yanagi, alongside renowned potters Shoji Hamada and Bernard Leach, they founded the Mingei movement, short for mingei undo, or "folk craft movement." Their goal was not just to preserve rural Japanese crafts, but to elevate the humble, everyday object as something worthy of attention, care and beauty.

The movement emerged as a response to mechanization, which threatened to erase centuries of skill, variation and human touch. Yanagi believed that beauty lived not in perfection, but rather that: "The beauty of use is the truest beauty."

Thanks to the efforts of the Mingei movement, crafts like pottery, weaving and woodworking regained their cultural status in Japan, influencing generations of artists and makers around the world. Today, pottery has become an almost mainstream hobby, a symbol of intentional living, even in urban settings.

The Mingei philosophy of preservation and practice lives on, not only in museums, but in the hands and hearts of those who continue to make. One such example lies in the Uji tea country near Kyoto, where Matsubayashi Hosai XVI, the current master of Asahiyaki, continues a lineage of potters stretching back over 400 years. As the 16th generation in his family to shape clay into vessels for tea, he embodies the Mingei spirit, not only preserving tradition but guiding it to evolve with grace.

The Asahiyaki kiln has stayed rooted in its purpose, vessels for the tea ceremony, but it has never stopped innovating. Their traditional wood-fired kiln has been adapted to modern safety standards, carefully mended rather than replaced. Their aesthetics have evolved subtly to meet new contexts, yet their philosophy remains intact.

Visitors to the workshop are often mesmerised, not just by the beauty of the work, but by the atmosphere of quiet purpose. Speaking with Hosai is often described as healing; he is as much philosopher as potter, shaping thoughts as gently as he shapes clay.

Perhaps now is the time to create a new Mingei movement, one that spans borders, mediums and disciplines. A movement that asks: What do we stand to lose if we forget how to make things with our hands?

And also: *What might we gain if we remember?*

A Story from Rome: What We've Lost and What We Could Regain

Walk down Via Francesco Crispi in Rome, metres away from the wonderful Dorchester Collection Eden Hotel and you'll find a small shop with no loud branding, no marketing gimmicks, just a name: Bocache & Salvucci.

Step inside and you'll meet a shoemaker who takes his time. There's no rush to sell. No menu of options. No mention of price. Instead, he begins with a conversation. He asks questions about how you walk, what you wear, what you need. He tells you how the shoes are made: the hand-stitching, the sole that will mould to your foot, the form that will hold its shape for decades.

> *"These are shoes for life,"* he might say. *"And if anything happens, you can always bring them back. I'll repair them myself."*

Only after this ritual of explanation and trust does price enter the conversation. And yes, of course, it is expensive. But perhaps not so expensive when you consider that these shoes may last a lifetime and that each visit deepens a relationship between maker and wearer. This is the opposite of modern consumerism. It's personal, transparent, human. And it's a glimpse of the kind of world people are longing for, often without realizing it, a world the luxury hotel can play a key part in creating.

The Hotel as Cultural Counterbalance

A luxury hotel is uniquely positioned to counteract the alienation of modern consumption that we've been describing, not just because it offers comfort, but because it can offer meaningful experiences. Guests come to luxury spaces looking not only for rest, but for reflection, reconnection and a sense of inspiration. Seen this way, a hotel can become a sanctuary for craft and embodied knowledge, a space where guests are invited to rediscover the act of making. It can also serve as a platform to rebuild trust in human-scale production and as a catalyst for more sustainable and intentional ways of living.

This isn't about nostalgia, it's about reviving what we've lost. And in that process, helping to restore agency, understanding and connection in a world that is steadily stripping them away.

A Playbook for Reconnection

If hotels are to reclaim their role as cultural counterbalances, this vision has to be made practical. It must move from principle into practice, from abstract ideals into concrete offerings that touch daily guest life. That's where the playbook begins, with a series of simple, tangible ways hoteliers can bring reconnection to life inside their walls, built around workshops and residencies.

At the core of this part of the playbook is the idea of offering immersive sessions where guests engage directly with skilled craftspeople, focusing on traditional and tactile techniques such as ceramics, throwing clay, glazing, or practising Japanese kintsugi; textiles, including hand-weaving, natural dyeing and visible mending; woodworking, such as carving spoons, plates, or small boxes; and even bookbinding and shoemaking. These sessions not only teach a skill, they reconnect people to materials, time and attention and help to restore confidence in the ability to use our hands, not just our minds.

In actuality, hotels have long been associated with crafts, particularly in traditional regions where demonstrations are often part of the guest experience. But in most cases, this remains symbolic or decorative. You might see a potter spinning a wheel in the lobby, or a weaver showcasing their loom, but you rarely see a working workshop on-site; no kilns, no full-size looms, no forges or dye vats. The infrastructure of real making is almost always absent.

Why? Because hotels, especially those in dense city centres, are always under pressure for space. And once a property is built, space is fully accounted for. You can't invent a ceramics studio once every room has been sold.

This means that the opportunity lies at the conception and design stage. It's at this point that a hotel must decide: is this a place that celebrates craft? If the answer is yes, then the commitment must be built into the foundations, allocating real space to fully functioning craft workshops and to artist studios with proper ventilation, light and tools. The point is not to just add a residency, but design for one. Ideally, a guest should be able to walk into a space and feel that it was built with the same care and clarity as the objects being made there. When this happens, the hotel is no longer just showing craft. It is living it. Supporting it not only as an experience for guests, but as a philosophy of how to build and maintain a space where making, meaning and hospitality co-exist in harmony.

This commitment naturally extends into a residency model, where local or international artisans are invited to live and work on-site, not as entertainers, but as practicing masters of their craft. Guests may visit their studios during the day, ask questions, observe their process, or join an occasional masterclass. Fundamentally, each artist or artisan would bring with them not only their techniques but also their story, philosophy and memory, helping to turn the hotel into a cultural laboratory of living heritage.

A potter shaping bowls while explaining the soil they were made from. A weaver telling the story of her grandmother's patterns. A woodworker inviting guests to help carve a communal table. This is not the mummified culture of a museum, but a living, breathing tradition of artists and artisans who invite guests to become part of their practice, rather than passive observers of it. Offerings like these aren't just activities. They are authentic encounters with people, place and purpose.

Together, full craft workshops and residencies create a layered cultural offering, where guests not only make but also observe and connect, engaging with craft on multiple levels, from hands-on practice to meaningful encounters with the people behind the work.

In the best cases, guests return, not just to stay, but to continue learning. To deepen the relationship with a place that invited them to slow down, touch something real and shape something lasting with their own two hands.

Craft-integrated Design and Storytelling

But reconnection need not stop with workshops or residencies; it can also be woven directly into the very fabric of the hotel itself, through the objects, materials and stories that shape its design.

The key here is to infuse the hotel's design with locally crafted objects, furnishing rooms, restaurants and lobbies with handmade furniture, textiles and ceramics. Each item carries a story, shared through a tag, a booklet, or even digital content, so that a guest might sleep under a quilt woven nearby or drink from a cup shaped just down the road. What matters is not the scale of these choices but their presence. Even a handful of thoughtfully chosen pieces can shift the atmosphere, reminding guests that the place they're staying is rooted in human hands and local stories.

A perfect example of this spirit lives in Kyoto, at the Hiiragiya ryokan, where we had the privilege of meeting Mrs. Nishimura, the sixth-generation host of this legendary inn. She shared stories not just of her guests, but of the craftspeople whose work lives inside each room.

In Room 52, the room discussed by Amina and Mr Leclerc at the start of this chapter, sits the tokonoma (decorative alcove) made by Kiyotsugu Nakagawa.[8] The wood flooring of the alcove utilises rare Jindai cryptomeria wood, unearthed from Mount Chōkai. Every piece of wood in the tokonoma fits together like a puzzle, joined not merely with tools, but through a sensitive alignment of wood grain, chosen and fitted with precision.

Mrs. Nishimura also explained that the ceiling is crafted from rare Yakusugi cedar, a highly prized wood sourced from ancient cedar trees on Yakushima Island. A wood so rare and flawless that it contains no knots. Why no knots? Because the craftspeople climb the trees and prune each new branch as it grows, year after year, generation after generation. It is an act of living patience, not just material selection.

The entire ryokan is alive with craft, just waiting to be discovered. It remains as discreet as a guest may want. It is only when a guest shows genuine interest that a conversation with Mrs. Nishimura might begin, slowly unfurling the many layers of excellence and intention involved in each piece of the inn.

This is what it truly means to integrate craft into design. Not as ornamentation or branding, but as living relationships, carried across generations, between makers, hosts and guests.

When a hotel is shaped by craft, its walls are not just walls. They become stories, relationships and invitations, to look closer, to feel more deeply and to take part in a culture where care has been built into the very architecture of hospitality.

Towards a Hospitality of Repair

Just as craft woven into a hotel's design reminds guests of human care and provenance, the act of repair offers another path to reconnection, showing that what is broken can not only be restored, but made more meaningful in the process.

In a world where replacement has become easier than repair, there is something radical and deeply reassuring, about mending what we already have. In our vision, a hotel committed to reconnection can reintroduce repair as a ritual, not just a service. For example, guests could be invited to bring personal items, clothing, broken objects, even shoes, for restoration. This doesn't require vast workshops or elaborate facilities, the scale is far less important than the gesture itself. Even a small offering, like inviting guests to bring personal items for mending, having a "Repair Concierge" on hand, or setting aside a modest "fix-it lounge" with tools and guides, can transform repair into both a practical and meaningful part of the stay.

We believe that this is about more than sustainability. It's about caring for what you own, understanding how things are made and restoring a sense of competence and stewardship. In this sense, repair becomes an act of resistance, against waste, against speed, against forgetting and equally, an act of transmission, passing on the skills and knowledge that allow future generations to keep making, mending and sustaining what matters.

Across Europe and beyond, we're already seeing signs of this movement, particularly in the form of bike repair cafés. These are not just workshops, they are often community spaces, combining tools and espresso, passion and hospitality. Examples include Steel Vintage Bikes in Berlin, La Chouette in Paris and The HandleBar in Oxford.

One of the best examples for many years was at the Relais Plaza in Paris, where restaurant manager Werner Küchler, a lifelong cycling enthusiast, used his love for bikes to connect with guests. He often rode with them, exchanged stories and built genuine relationships that began with wheels and turned into lifelong friendships. His story is a reminder: repair and passion can build true hospitality.

Just like mending a jacket or repairing a pot, fixing a bicycle becomes a gesture of love, for the object, for oneself and for a different way of being in the world.

This reintroduces a lost cultural norm, that broken things are not worthless. They're waiting to be restored and in that process, so are we. And perhaps, in that restoration, they become more beautiful.

We probably see this best in the Japanese art of kintsugi, where broken ceramics are repaired with gold and where these marks of care become part of the object's story. Its wounds are not hidden but honoured. The item is not simply returned to what it was, it becomes more meaningful, more whole and more human because it has been broken and lovingly repaired.

Reflective Programming & Slow Philosophy

Repair, then, is not just about objects, rather it points us back to deeper questions of value, memory and meaning. And this is where hotels can take the next step, moving from the practice of repair into reflective programming that helps guests explore what these acts say about how we live, what we cherish and what we've lost.

Crucial to this kind of programming is going beyond physical objects and inviting guests to reflect on the meaning behind them. Hotels might create guided experiences that pair craft with conversation, or host evening salons with thinkers, artisans, designers and cultural historians. These gatherings could explore themes such as "The Value of Things," "What We've Forgotten," or "How to Live With Our Hands Again," turning a stay into not just a retreat, but a thoughtful encounter with ideas that linger long after departure. A stay that nourishes not only the body, mind and soul, but stays in the hands as embodied knowledge.

Conclusion

In this chapter we have traced not only the disquieting outlines of the crisis of disconnection that defines our age, but also the subtle ways in which our material reality too feels like it is slipping beyond our reach. This is a world where most people no longer know how the things around them are made, repaired, or sustained. A world where people rarely meet those who help to build the objects that help us as individuals and societies, survive and even thrive.

This loss has created not only a kind of dependence on processes, people and machines far away, but also an underlying sense of anxiety and helplessness which continues to erode the deep sense of meaning we have always entrusted to the material world. And yet, we have also seen how craft, whether through bookbinding, shoemaking, or even the daily act of cooking, retains a powerful antidote to this disconnection and disquiet. By forging anew the connections between people and between people and objects, it helps to restore trust, reawaken awe and remind us that human touch, patience and skill can make life not only more beautiful but more sustainable.

We believe that hotels can act as counterweights for those forces pulling us apart, as sanctuaries for reconnection, craft and meaning. By weaving a myriad of traditional forms of making into their design, offering residencies and workshops and even embracing the philosophy of repair, they have the chance to counterbalance the alienation of modern life with deeply-rooted encounters that are memorable, meaningful and restorative. This is not nostalgia. Nor is it new age idealism. It's a strategy that provides exceptional and sustainable experiences that help bring guests back to a place they feel at home in, time and time again.

CHAPTER SEVEN

Food for thought

This final chapter is both a conclusion and a provocation. Much of this book has been concerned with how hospitality can respond to a changing world – overcrowding, distraction, miswanting, environmental strain – and still offer something coherent, meaningful and human. Food is where these questions converge.

It is not only one of the areas where luxury hospitality will be most tested in the years ahead; it is also where many of its greatest opportunities lie. For what happens at the table shapes not just guest satisfaction, but the climate, the landscape, the economies of our regions and, ultimately, the meaning of what it is to live well together.

Food has a particular clarity. It arrives on a trolley, lands on a plate, and is judged in seconds. It makes visible the choices that are otherwise easy to abstract: how a hotel relates to craft and care, to labour and land, to waste and attention. In food, the hotel's values are no longer theoretical. They are tasted.

It is tempting to think of food (and beverage) as just a department: breakfast, banqueting, restaurant, room service, minibar. But food is not merely an operational function. It is one of the clearest expressions of what a hotel stands for. It is where care becomes tangible. Where supply chains meet story, and where a hotel's relationship to culture, skill and stewardship becomes hard to disguise.

And because everyone eats – regardless of age, nationality, ideology or budget – food is one of the few parts of hospitality that every guest experiences directly. You can redesign a lobby and some guests won't notice. You can change the pillow menu and many won't care. But if breakfast feels anonymous, if ingredients feel unconsidered, if the dining room feels rushed or performative, guests sense it immediately. Food is where luxury either becomes real or reveals its superficiality.

The Breakfast Test

Consider breakfast, the most unglamorous battleground in a luxury hotel.

At 8:00 a.m. the room is already full. There is a queue at the door. Someone is negotiating with a small child. A guest in athleisure photographs chia pudding beside a carefully angled cappuccino. A business traveller scans emails between bites. A couple who arrived late surveys what remains and looks faintly disappointed.

Breakfast, in other words, is modern life compressed into a single hour.

It is also where a hotel's choices show. Do we offer abundance at any cost, flying in fruit out of season and building buffets designed for excess, much of which will be thrown away? Do we staff thinly and hope the guest forgives the friction? Or do we design a breakfast that feels coherent: seasonal where it can be, generous where it should be, calm where it matters, and staffed by people who are not rushing past guests like traffic?

Food is where a hotel's internal pressures – labour shortages, volatile costs, fragile supply chains – collide with the guest's need for ease, comfort and meaning. That collision is not going away. It is one of the defining operational realities of the coming decade.

Why Food Brings Everything Together

Throughout this book, we have argued that hospitality must evolve. The old model – provide service, provide opulence, meet expectations, exceed them where possible – is no longer sufficient on its own. The world is more strained, more distracted and more sceptical.

Guests want generosity and simplicity, comfort and virtue, novelty and authenticity. Staff want meaning and growth, but also stability, pay and lives that are workable. Communities want tourism's revenue without its extraction. And the planet is making the cost of business as usual increasingly difficult to ignore.

Food.

It is a craft, requiring skill and judgment. It is a training ground, revealing whether a hotel invests in people or burns them out. It is a cultural interface, connecting guests to place, or severing that connection. It is a systems problem, where waste and procurement are either designed out or quietly compounded. And it is a story, whether we choose to tell it or not.

That is why we end here. Not to moralise about what people should eat, but because food is an honest mirror. It shows whether a hotel is simply delivering a product or stewarding an experience worth sustaining.

A Brief Look Back

We began this book with overcrowding: how success can hollow out the very places that make travel meaningful. Food is part of that story. When destinations become stage sets, dining cultures often flatten with them. Menus lose specificity. Producers are squeezed. Guests end up eating an expensive version of something they could have had anywhere.

We then turned to staffing. Food sits at the centre of this challenge. Kitchens and restaurants are among the most demanding parts of any hotel, and often the first place where shortages are felt. When food teams are treated as endlessly replaceable, quality declines, costs rise and service becomes transactional. When teams are trained, supported and proud of their craft, food becomes one of the strongest expressions of a hotel's identity.

We looked at distraction and presence. Food can amplify distraction – rushed service, loud rooms, an atmosphere designed for performance, dishes designed merely to be photographed – or it can counter it. A well-paced meal slows time. A shared table creates conversation. A dining room designed for presence restores a rhythm that many guests have lost.

We explored miswanting: the chase for novelty, status, and "more", even when it leaves people unsatisfied. Food is one of the most common sites of miswanting in modern life. Hospitality can choose not to amplify it. Taste beats excess. Provenance beats spectacle. The most memorable dish is rarely the most expensive one; it is the one that feels carefully thought about.

Finally, we explored estrangement: how modern life pulls people away from craft and from the origins of what they consume. Food is one of the simplest ways to bring people back, not through explanation, but through experience.

Setting the Scene: Food and the Good Life

For the good life to remain possible in this century, we may need to learn to live in ways that place less strain on the world around us. The climate crisis makes this unavoidable, and food is one of the areas where its consequences are most immediate. What and how we eat shapes emissions, landscapes and supply chains built into modern food systems.

Hotels can respond through formal sustainability initiatives, and they should. But hospitality also exerts a quieter form of influence. Hotels and restaurants have always helped define what a good life looks like – not through argument, but through experience. They persuade by pleasure.

This is why we advocate centring food around plants. Not as a demand for purity, nor an expectation that everyone eat the same way, but because the world needs many people to eat a little differently. When plant-forward food is generous, satisfying and well made, it does not feel like compromise. It feels like refinement.

Before considering what hotels can do, it is worth being honest about the world guests are arriving from. Over the last decade, plant-based eating has been highly visible in media, conferences and menus. And yet adoption in much of Europe and the United States has plateaued. Most people say they want to eat more plants, but relatively few do so consistently.

This gap is not a failure of information. The headline arguments are widely known. Habits are hard to shift in a world that is time-poor, convenience-driven and increasingly distracted.

Since COVID, convenience has accelerated further. Food delivery has become infrastructure. Takeaway has become default. While this has expanded access to global cuisines, it has also increased food's footprint through transport, fragmented logistics and packaging waste. At the same time, home cooking – the skill base on which food culture depends – has been eroding in many urban households. Kitchens shrink. Work bleeds into evenings. People eat alone more often. Cooking from scratch begins to feel like an unreasonable demand rather than a normal part of life.

As a result, many guests arrive at hotels with a distinctly modern combination: strong opinions about food and limited practical agency around it. They may care about sustainability or health, but struggle to act on those values day to day. They may also associate plant-forward eating with compromise or joylessness, not because it is so, but because that is how it has often been framed.

In much of Europe and the United States, this framing is reinforced by menu design itself. Vegetarian and vegan dishes are frequently segregated or marked in ways that subtly signal "otherness." However well intentioned, these cues imply substitution rather than desirability. Something you order if you must, not because you want to.

The cultural headwinds differ by region. In much of Asia, Africa, and the Middle East, plant-forward food is rooted in tradition rather than trend. In contrast, much of Europe and especially the United States has built its mainstream food culture around meat as centrepiece, not only nutritionally, but symbolically. Steak, barbecue, Sunday roasts and indulgence remain tightly linked in the imagination.

For luxury hotels serving international guests, this context matters. The opportunity is not to persuade through argument, but to demonstrate through pleasure. If plant-forward dishes are treated as side options, guests will read them as compromise. If they are designed as the best dishes on the menu – seasonal, generous, deeply flavoured – guests choose them because they are good.

Design Beats Ideology

This is why the future of food in hospitality is less about purity than about re-centring. Making plants more central, not as identity, but as practice. Not substitutes, but standards.

What we are advocating is food that stands on its own terms: dishes that happen to be plant-based because that is what makes them most delicious.

Many of the world's most beloved dishes already provide the foundation. They were never branded as plant-based. These traditional dishes are simply good: slow-cooked legumes, vegetable stews, spice-rich curries, pasta dishes where meat is accent rather than foundation. Hotels can reclaim and elevate this rich culinary inheritance, preparing it with local ingredients and seasonality, without turning the dining room into a debate.

The same logic applies to waste and procurement. Guests do not need lectures. They respond to coherence. Menus designed around availability. Techniques that use ingredients fully. Purchasing built on local relationships rather than anonymity. These are operational decisions, not moral statements, but guests feel the difference.

Food as Transmission

Food is one of the most natural bridges between guests and place. It is culture you can eat.

Transmission does not require grand programmes. Often it works best when it is lightly offered: a short conversation with someone who knows the story, a tasting that reveals a local ingredient, a small ritual that slows the meal. These moments give guests something rare. Not just service, but a sense that their time was well spent.

This matters because many guests arrive hungry for more than comfort. They want an experience that feels grounded and real. Food can give them that, not by demanding participation, but by inviting it.

Beyond the Plate

Food is not the only arena where hospitality will be tested in the years ahead, but it is one of the clearest. It is where cost, labour, culture, community, and sustainability collide – daily, visibly, and without abstraction.

What makes food especially powerful, however, is not only what happens in the dining room, but what happens afterwards.

At its best, hospitality does more than satisfy needs in the moment. It leaves guests with something they can carry forward. That their choices were not neutral. That they were participants rather than passive consumers. This is where food, quietly and effectively, builds agency.

Agency does not need explanation. It is felt. When a menu reflects real relationships with growers, when a dish makes use of ingredients that would otherwise be wasted, when a meal is paced in a way that restores attention rather than fragments it, guests intuit that their presence has consequences, in a meaningful, not burdensome way.

These moments need not be grand. A short cooking session focused on seasonal vegetables may change how someone cooks at home. A conversation about a regenerative vineyard may shape future wine choices. A breakfast that feels calm and intentional may subtly recalibrate what "enough" feels like. Through food, hotels can transform consumption into contribution and indulgence into participation.

This is not about asking guests to be better people. It is about designing experiences that make better choices feel natural, and even pleasurable. When done well, guests don't feel instructed. They feel empowered.

And this is where the scale of hospitality begins to matter.

No single menu or hotel will change food culture on its own. At first, these choices may barely be noticed. But over time, they accumulate, they take root, they multiply, shaping habits and norms. What begins as a sourcing decision or a menu design becomes a signal. What works quietly spreads.

For hoteliers, this means recognising that choices made at property level are not merely operational. They are cultural contributions. They express a belief about what hospitality is for, and what kind of life it supports.

This work is not easy. There is inertia, resistance and pressure to revert to familiar models of luxury. But there is also opportunity: to create spaces where a more thoughtful way of eating and living is framed not as sacrifice, but as refinement. Not as ideology, but as pleasure. Not as denial, but as abundance.

Seen this way, food is not an isolated concern. It is a microcosm of hospitality itself. Every choice – what we serve, how we source, how we train, how we invite guests into experience – carries consequences that extend beyond the stay.

The future of the luxury hotel is unwritten. But like every meal, it begins with a choice.

CHECK OUT

A few words before you check out.

If you are closing this book, it means you've stayed with us for a while. Long enough, perhaps, to see yourself in its pages. Long enough to reflect on what it means to keep our craft as hoteliers alive in a time of noise, scarcity and strain. Long enough to remember that hospitality, if done well, is never only a business. It's a way of caring for the world and its people.

This has been a journey through multiple crises and possibilities. Overcrowding, understaffing, disconnection, miswanting, unmet needs and the quiet estrangement from the very things we touch. These are not light burdens. They weigh on our teams, our guests and on each of us. But they are also fissures, cracks through which, with creativity and determination, we can let a little light in.

What have we found on this journey?

That hospitality carries extraordinary power.

That it has a powerful agency, helping to remind guests their choices matter, that luxury can be an act of contribution, not only of consumption.

That it can act as a powerful counterweight, providing sanctuaries of presence, story and care within a myriad of places and communities, helping to hold us steady against the different forces of modern life that act to pull us apart.

And that these special places we steward have the potential to not just sustain, but to actively renew places, people and practices.

Paradoxically, this work of hospitality we do together is both humble and ambitious. It starts small, not everything all at once, in already fertile soil. Perhaps it begins with a real need met with thought and care, or a meal designed to nourish without waste. But with attention it can grow to something much larger than ourselves.

So, as you check out, remember: this book was not here to fix you or your practice, nor to offer easy solutions, but rather to walk beside you as a friend might. To offer questions worth carrying home. To remind you that your work, even on the hardest days, is significant and even sacred.

And obviously hospitality will never save the world alone. But it can help nurture some of those parts that matter most. And in a century defined by distraction, disconnection and ecological destruction, that may be one of the most hopeful contributions anyone can make.

Now we end as we began, reminding you that this has been a love letter.

To the owner who nurtures their vision of the future, holding both risk and possibility so that others may thrive.
To the general manager who steadies the ship, calmly navigating a thousand unseen challenges and keeping everyone onboard.
To the restaurateur who writes stories in flavour, reminding us that meals are more than sustenance.
And to all those who carry the weighty pieces of this craft each day, choosing, again and again, to make care your calling.

This is what you do. This is what we all do. It's who we are.

The house is still open.

Safe travels. Come back any time.

ENDNOTES

1 Using, co2.myclimate.org/en/flight_calculators/new.
Other studies estimate closer to 200 kg CO2e per round trip, depending on calculation method, distance and aircraft efficiency.

2 Based on analysis from circularecology.com regarding the carbon emissions associated with hotel stays.

3 Kuo-Tsang Huang, Jen Chun Wang, Yi-Chieh Wang (2015)
Analysis and benchmarking of greenhouse gas emissions of luxury hotels. International Journal of Hospitality Management 51. pp. 56-66. doi.org/10.1016/j.ijhm.2015.08.014.

4 Each year, the city welcomes around 21 million visitors, despite having a population of just 883,000.

5 These examples also remind us that while hosts can set the stage for presence, guests must choose to step onto it. We believe that hospitality only truly flourishes only when both sides lean in; not only when the hotelier has the courage to draw boundaries, but when the guest has the willingness to accept them.

6 In particular Mistakenly Seeking Solitude from the Journal of Experimental Psychology.

7 As we discussed earlier, a hygiene factor is something that prevents dissatisfaction when present but does not, on its own, create lasting satisfaction or joy.

8 Nakagawa is a renowned Japanese woodworker designated as a Living National Treasure, a title given in Japan to those who have mastered and preserved traditional arts at the highest level.

Company examples throughout the book are used illustratively. Interpretations reflect the authors' perspective and are not intended as definitive historical or commercial assessments.

A SPACE FOR NOTES

ABOUT THE AUTHORS

Philippe Krenzer and Jannes Sörensen were long-time friends and colleagues who worked together in the luxury hospitality industry over many years and shared an ethos and a vision.

Philippe managed some of the world's most beautiful hotels, including the Four Seasons in London and Chicago, The Ritz, The Savoy and Claridge's in London, the Hôtel de Crillon in Paris, the Oberoi in Bali, and the Omni in Hong Kong. In 2005, Philippe launched Philippe Krenzer and Associates (PKA) specialising in luxury hospitality, consulting, and training. He was also Professor of Service Strategy MBA at HEC Paris, visiting Professor of Strategy at Les Roches International School of Hotel Management in Switzerland and Founding Academic Lead at KIHA. Philippe passed away in late October 2025.

Jannes joined Jeremy King's Beaumont Hotel in London early 2016, becoming one of the UK's youngest general managers. Over the next five years, he elevated the hotel into an award-winning destination, earning numerous accolades and being named World's Best General Manager two years in a row.

At the heart of his success is a philosophy rooted in building meaningful relationships with guests and co-workers alike – believing excellence naturally follows. Jannes started his journey as a concierge, working his way up with roles at the world's most prestigious five-star hotels, including the Kempinski Hotel Adlon in Berlin, the Four Seasons George V in Paris, the Ritz-Carlton Hotel Arts in Barcelona, The Plaza Hotel in New York City, The Connaught in London and Le Bristol in Paris. He has a Master Certificate in the Essentials of Hospitality Management from Cornell University. In 2023, he launched Kepler Hotel Group, and set up a highly selective hospitality academy. Kepler International Hospitality Academy (KIHA) focuses on methods and ideas for creating a positive impact on the world, in tandem with a deep attunement to human needs.

www.ingramcontent.com/pod-product-compliance
Ingram Content Group UK Ltd.
Pitfield, Milton Keynes, MK11 3LW, UK
UKHW040935080626
12970UKWH00038B/217